DIVING AND SNORKELING GUIDE TO

The Hawaiian Islands

by Doug Wallin
and the editors of Pisces Books

Pisces Books
A Division of Gulf Publishing Company
Houston, Texas

Series Editor: Steve Blount

Photos: All photos are by the author, unless otherwise noted.

Library of Congress Cataloging in Publication Data
Wallin, Doug.
   Diving and snorkeling guide to the Hawaiian Islands.
   Bibliography: p.
   1. Skin diving—Hawaii—Guide-books. 2. Scuba diving—Hawaii—Guide-books. I. Title. GV840.S782U68
1984   797.2′3′09969   84-1079
ISBN 1-55992-003-3

Reprinted May 1989

Printed in Hong Kong

10   9   8   7   6   5   4

Table of Contents

How to Use This Guide

This book provides information that both resident and visitor to Hawaii can use when evaluating snorkel and scuba diving locations on the four major Hawaiian islands of Oahu, Maui, the Big Island of Hawaii, and Kauai. Descriptions for each dive site include typical water conditions, depths, recommended entries and exits, what can you expect to see in the way of topography and marine life, the necessary skill level, and more. Such information should help you evaluate whether a particular site is appropriate for your desires and abilities.

For newcomers to Hawaii, and even for experienced divers, it is strongly recommended that initial snorkel and scuba excursions be made with a dive shop or dive tour company. You must realize that dive sites from one area of an island to another can vary greatly in diveability due to the differing wind, water, current, and weather conditions that can exist around an island at any given time. During the winter months, for instance, diving can be treacherous on the north shore of any island because of heavy ocean swells and surf, even while the leeward and other coastal areas may offer calm waters and beautiful diving conditions.

If you decide to go snorkeling or scuba diving on your own rather than with an organized tour, be sure to study your intended dive site carefully. Consult a dive shop in the area to check recent weather and water conditions. If the spot you have chosen hasn't been good lately, most shops can suggest a better one and save you the wasted time of going to unfavorable and possibly hazardous location.

The Rating System for Divers and Dives

Our suggestions as to the minimum level of expertise required for any given dive should be taken in a conservative sense, keeping in mind the old adage about there being old divers and bold divers but few old bold divers. We consider a *novice* to be someone in decent physical condition, who has recently completed a basic certification diving course, or a certified diver who has not been diving recently or who has no experience in similar waters. We consider an *intermediate* to be a certified diver in excellent physical condition who has been diving actively for at least a year following a basic course, and who has been diving recently in similar waters. We consider an *advanced* diver to be someone who has completed an advanced certification diving course, has been diving recently in similar waters, and is in excellent physical condition. You will have to decide if you are capable of making any particular dive, depending on your level of training, recency of experience, and physical condition, as well as water conditions at the site. Remember that water conditions can change at any time, even during a dive.

The recommended diving sites in Hawaii are presented in four chapters, one for each island. Locations have been chosen to provide the full gamut of underwater experiences from easily accessible shallow-water reefs teeming with tropical fish to cave diving, wreck diving, and night diving. Sites have also been chosen to include both snorkel and scuba diving locations that can satisfy everyone from the novice skin diver to the long-time scuba enthusiast.

Hawaii's sky-blue waters promise much and deliver more to the diver and snorkeler. All types of watersports are the favored recreation at Waikiki Beach, in the shadow of the volcano Diamond Head.

1

Overview of the Hawaiian Islands

The Hawaiian Islands represent the northernmost extent of Polynesia, which means "many islands." The area is also referred to as the Polynesian triangle, which extends from New Zealand, northeast to Hawaii, and southeast to Easter Island. Hawaii itself is the most isolated archipelago in the world, over 2000 miles (3200 kilometers) from the nearest major land mass. This, along with the fact that these islands are contained in only 6500 square miles (16,640 square kilometers) of land area, explains why Hawaii was one of the last major island chains in the Pacific to be populated.

The Early Polynesians. The origin of the Polynesians, of whom the Hawaiians are a part, is even today somewhat questionable and research is still going on. Much of the difficulty in determining their origin stems from the fact that the Polynesians never developed a written language. As a result, their history was recorded through a system of elaborate narrative chants. It is very difficult to put events in chronological order using only the information recorded in such chants, where time is measured by generations and the length of reigns of chiefs instead of years. It was not until 1821, when American missionaries first arrived in the islands, that a Hawaiian alphabet and written language was developed. A great effort was then made by the missionaries to write down as much historical knowledge as could be learned from the islanders.

Polynesians are imaginative people, and tales of gods, demons, and supernatural events permeate their lore. Thus, it is often hard to separate fact from fiction.

It has not been until recently, in fact, that modern scientific methods have been evolved to help study the past. Such disciplines as linguistics, carbon dating, archaeology, and anthropology have greatly aided the determination of the history of the Polynesians. Today, this story is fairly complete and accurate, encompassing events from the birth of the Polynesian race to the present.

Isolated by over 2000 miles of ocean, the Hawaiian Islands went undiscovered for more than 250 years after Europeans began exploring the Pacific. ▶

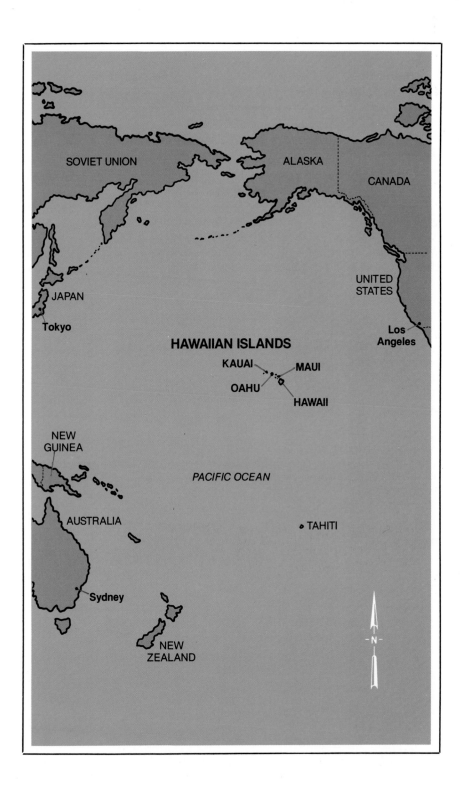

SOVIET UNION

ALASKA

CANADA

JAPAN

UNITED
STATES

Tokyo

Los
Angeles

HAWAIIAN ISLANDS

KAUAI

MAUI

OAHU

HAWAII

NEW
GUINEA

PACIFIC OCEAN

AUSTRALIA

TAHITI

Sydney

NEW
ZEALAND

-N-

7

The Islands Today

Oahu. Oahu is the main island in the Hawaiian chain; the name means "the gathering place," which is appropriate because Honolulu is the state capital and Oahu holds most of Hawaii's over one million residents. Honolulu has blossomed into one of the major business crossroads of the world. Tourism is undeniably the state's leading industry, with over three million visitors winging their way in and out each year—more than 3 times the entire resident population coming and going every 12 months. Oahu is also home to Waikiki's glittering "miracle mile."

As the population center of the state, Oahu is the most developed island industrially—and that includes the tourist industry. The great majority of hotel and condominium accommodations are located in or very near Waikiki and its strands of golden sand beaches. Within the Waikiki/Honolulu area you will find a vast array of souvenir and gift shops, famous restaurants serving international cuisine, movie theaters, stage show and night clubs, luaus, and much more. There is also Ala Moana shopping center, one of the largest shopping complexes in the world, selling everything anyone could ever hope to buy. All Oahu is serviced by a good bus system and a plethora of tour companies, so a rental car is by no means mandatory. There are numerous dive shops around Oahu as well as dozens of dive tour and diving equipment rental companies to handle all your diving needs. To put it simply, in the state of Hawaii Oahu is where it's happening.

Hawaii was settled by Polynesians, who arrived in the 8th century A.D. aboard voyaging canoes like this replica, built by the Polynesian Voyaging Society.

An actor in the Kodak Hula Show portraying King Kamehameha the Great wears a cape similar to those worn by early Hawaiian rulers. Such capes were made from the feathers of as many as 80,000 birds.

Sightseeing. A hike through the lush green rain forest of Manoa Valley is highly recommended. Literally translated the name means Rainbow Valley, and it is a popular local spot. The valley is the one right behind Honolulu. Follow the signs into Manoa and you'll find Paradise Park, another interesting attraction in its own right. The road narrows beyond the park, soon becoming a dirt road and then ending in a trail. This trail winds for about a mile (1½ kilometers) through Manoa's primordial rain forest, ending at the headwaters of a spectacular double waterfall.

For something really different, try the glider plane rides at Mokuleia, on Oahu's north shore.

Two other places hold particular interest for those who like the ocean and the creatures that inhabit it. At the far east end of Waikiki, just below Diamond Head, is the Waikiki Aquarium; on the far eastern edge of the Oahu coast is Makapuu Point, home of Sea Life Park.

Great Restaurants. Gastronomically speaking, Oahu is a glutton's delight. Within a very small area can be found restaurants featuring menus from all over the world. For elegant (and expensive) dining try the French restaurant Bistro behind Diamond Head, or John Dominis overlooking the ocean in Honolulu. Economical, but excellent, food is found at Ray's Seafood in the Waikiki shopping plaza. A popular family coffee shop and lounge frequented by locals is the Columbia Inn, on Kapiolani Blvd. in Honolulu. For the best in Chinese fare, and quite reasonably priced, visit McCully Chop Suey on the corner of McCully and King Streets. If you journey to the north shore, two excellent places are the Crouching Lion and the Proud Peacock restaurant in Waimea Falls Park.

Maui

After Oahu, Maui is the most visited island in the Hawaiian chain. In fact, many returning visitors to the island bypass Honolulu all together and head straight for Maui. Many residents and visitors agree that Maui is *no ka oi* (the best).

Maui is divided geographically and geologically into two lobes, actually two volcanic mountain tops, which merge into East and West Maui. The action on the island is located on the leeward shores, the three main centers being Kihei/Wailea on East Maui and Lahaina and Kaanapali on West Maui.

Second only to Waikiki as a tourist mecca, Kaanapali beach and resort complex is located west of Lahaina and stretches for several miles around the western perimeter of the island to the luxury resort area of Kapalua. Kihei, a 45-minute drive from Lahaina to the east, is also a developed visitor resort area but on a scale much less frenetic than Kaanapali. If you like to be in the thick of things, enjoy fine cuisine in the elegant surroundings, and in general like to keep one hand on the pulse of civilization, Kaanapali is the place to stay. If, on the other hand, you wish the amenities of the modern world to be tempered with a more countryish atmosphere, Kikei should be your base of operations.

The coasts of the islands are littered with small volcanic outcroppings like Rabbit Island. Often, the reefs near them are honeycombed with lava tube caverns.

The yellow goatfish wears different colors at night than it does during the day. Colorful tropical species of all kinds is one thing that makes Hawaii special.

Lahaina. One of the unique above-water attractions of Maui is historic Lahaina town. Lahaina was the capital of Hawaii long before Honolulu. In the mid-19th century it was the hub of the once great Pacific whaling industry, a seaport town where rowdy sea-roughened sailors caroused along narrow streets, frequently getting thrown in jail by missionaries whenever they became too unruly. Today Lahaina is a place where the past lives into the present: a hundred years back Hawaiian history with all the comforts of the modern world.

Hotels and Restaurants. Maui's natural creations are free to enjoy, but not so those built by man. Be prepared for Maui: it is not a cheap. Kaanapali to Kapalua hotels and condos are expensive; Kihei and Wailea somewhat less so. If you wish for economy, the Travel Lodge and Pioneer Inn in Lahaina are small, informal, clean, and relatively inexpensive. If you wish to stay in Kaanapali itself, but still with an eye on economy, the Kaanapali Beach Hotel is one of the better bargains on the beach.

As in most places, the cost of hotel food tends to be high. One of the best bargains around for breakfast is the restaurant at the Travel Lodge. The omelettes are great, and half the price of other places. For breakfast, lunch, and dinner, oddly named Moose McGilicudys on Front Street in Lahaina serves delicious, huge meals for reasonable prices. The Rusty Harpoon on Kaanapali Beach has excellent barbeque-your-own dinners, prices moderate. Casual La Familia Mexican Restaurant in Kihei and Tortilla Flats in Lahaina can't be beat for all-around prices and food quality. For more elegant yet affordable dining, Kapalua Grill and Bar offers spectacular ocean scenery and fine cuisine. And don't miss the Hyatt Hotel's bar, which can be entered by an underground swimming pool!

The Big Island of Hawaii

After Maui, in terms of commercial development and as a visitor destination, comes the Big Island. Just that, the Big Island is the largest island in the Hawaiian chain. Also named Hawaii, the Big Island was so named so as to distinguish it from the other islands in the chain. Without a doubt, the Big Island offers the most varied above-water scenery in the state. If you come during the winter months, you can spend part of the day on the warm tropical beaches, then in the afternoon drive up the volcanic mountain of Mauna Kea and do some snow skiing.

Hilo. Hilo is not the visitor destination Kona is, nor is it intended to be. Hilo is much more rural and a large residential area. On the windward side of the island, Hilo gets the brunt of the tradewinds all year, and the idyllic calm South Seas beaches characteristic of the leeward side are missing. However, it is a gorgeous area to visit, and there are some very nice hotels and restaurants at some of the best prices in the state.

Hilo's Liluiokalani Gardens Park is a botanical and landscape extravaganza. A recommended hotel is the decidedly scenic Sheraton Waiakea Village hotel with its rooms, restaurants, lounges, and a shopping arcade built around tropical pools and palm-fringed ponds. For all-you-can-eat-and-drink Sunday champagne brunch, don't miss the Naniloa Surf hotel.

Kona. Kona is where the main thrust of the Big Island's visitor industry is located. This island is not known for its beaches; there are some nice ones, but they are infrequent. Most of the Big Island diving is done by boat. If you stay in Kona proper, a very nice hotel, with its own beach, is the King Kamehameha. A number of dive shops and underwater tour boat companies are located within a few blocks. South of Kona is the Keauhou Bay area featuring some nice hotels and condos, with several dive tour boat companies to serve you. Stretching up the volcanic rocky coastline north of Kona to Puako are a number of isolated hotels and resorts where you can really get away from it all. Such spots as the Kona Village Resort, Sheraton Royal Waikaloa, and the fabulous Mauna Kea Beach Hotel are built on gorgeous beaches and offer terrific diving that can be set up through the hotel activity desks.

The redish squirrelfish, like squirrelfish the world over, is a shy creature which prefers night to day. It's large eyes help it to see in the dark. ▶

Kauai

Kauai is the island where people go to get away from it all. Lushly green Kauai is considered by many to be the most beautiful island in the Hawaiian chain.

Visitors arrive at the quiet little airport in residential Lihue. Lihue is not, and is not intended to be, a visitor destination. It merely serves as an arrival place; visitors immediately move to Poipu to the south or Kapaa and Hanalei to the north.

Kapaa is more a residential town where some hotels and the Coconut Plantation shopping village have been built to entertain visitors. Some very nice, very reasonably priced hotels are found in Kapaa. The beaches are nice, but don't offer much in the way of diving.

Sightseeing. The real visitor meccas on Kauai are found on the north shore of Hanalie/Princeville and the south shore of Poipu.

The north shore, of course, catches more weather. It does have some excellent diving sites, but due to the sometimes quickly varying moods of wind and water, it is best to go with a dive tour to dive safely. The island's best, easiest, nearly year-round dive sites are found on the leeward southern shore. The beaches of Poipu are gorgeous and you will find the greatest variety of hotel and condo accommodations, as well as a plethora of dive shops, skin and scuba tour and equipment rental outfits. Above water Kauai offers a truly varied range of activities and sightseeing. It is an excellent place for visitors who have a mixture of divers and non-divers in their group. While the old salts are down under, there will always be something to keep the landlubbers busy and occupied.

Diving in Hawaii

Within Hawaii's sun warmed shallows, Nature has put on a truly breathtaking display of one of its most ambitious and prolific creations—the teeming world of the coral reef. Hawaii offers the full gamut of underwater experiences: cave and wall diving, night diving, spearfishing, and drift diving. Hawaii even boasts its own "ghost fleet"; scattered across the reef floor of many isles are numerous sunken wrecks—ships, boats, and planes—sent to a watery grave by World War II or by storms and other maritime mishaps.

Water Conditions. Hawaiian shores feel the brunt of all kinds of wind, wave, and water conditions. Currents are perhaps the greatest concern. Some diving areas, particularly those on the leeward coasts, are almost always free of any noticeable currents; other areas may be plagued practically all year. The Hawaiian Islands are relatively young, geologically speaking, and the corals have not yet had time to build up protective fringing reefs. Without these natural breakwaters, many shorelines are pounded by the full fury of the Pacific.

Many excellent diving and snorkeling sites can be found within swimming distance of the islands' golden beaches.

A variety of gear rental and diving tour services are available in the islands. While many sites can be dived without guides, some, such as Molokini Crater off Maui, require a boat with a knowledgeable captain.

Wind. Wind direction plays a vital role in determining day-to-day diving conditions. Eighty percent of the time the trade winds blow from the northeast, and the calmer waters of leeward coastlines generally make for the best year-round diving. A word of caution, however: the wind shadow generally extends only a few hundred yards (two or three hundred meters) offshore, where the trades once again hit the water and produce a surface current that flows out to sea. When you make a beach dive, be sure to leave sufficient air to enable you to swim back inside the wind shadow before you surface. In the winter months (November to April), the trades sometimes die and are replaced by southerly Kona winds. The strength of these winds has a profound effect on diving areas, especially those on the leeward coasts. When the Kona winds gust up from the south, high surf makes these areas undiveable. When the trades are replaced by Kona weather, dives flock to the windward side to log some bottom time during the temporary calm. Occasionally the Konas are very weak (less than five knots) and tranquil waters prevail almost everywhere.

The yellow tang, a cousin of the more common blue tang, brightens the waters of Molokini Crater. The fish in this protected park are almost tame.

On several islands the land forms protective wind shadows on the north shore areas, and during most of the year these waters are calm and extremely popular among underwater enthusiasts. In the winter, however, the north shores become home to giant surf, and a number of treacherous rips and undertows make diving hazardous. Dives should then be restricted to more protected locales.

Long-time island divers familiar with such perversities of wind, weather, and water know where and when to dive certain spots. If you are new to Hawaiian waters, you need to acquaint yourself with the variable conditions in order to maximize your enjoyment and diving safety.

Drop-offs. The well-defined ledges that run parallel to shore are one of the most notable underwater features to be found around many of the islands. They are called drop-offs and are located anywhere from near the shore to several hundred yards (two or three hundred meters or more) out. Such drop-offs create interesting topography, with steep walls cut by spectacular ravines, dramatic caves, and huge grottos that bustle with marine life.

Sport Diving Options

There are two ways to explore Hawaii's underwater realm: on your own or with a dive charter tour. A complete range of tour packages is available on most islands, from the normal half-day and full-day beach or boat excursions to special overnight or extended tours aboard larger dive vessels. All scuba divers who want to rent gear, fill tanks, or join a dive tour must present a certification card. No type of certification, however, is necessary to rent or purchase skin diving gear (mask, snorkel and fins) or to participate in snorkel tours.

Scuba Diving. If you have never been scuba diving there are two ways to get started. You can take what is called a resort introduction to scuba if your time is limited; this is a quick half-day lesson followed by an underwater tour with a professional diving guide. It's an inexpensive way to get a taste of scuba diving and see if you are interested in taking a complete certification course. For those with a little more time, dive shops and scuba tour companies offer special, individually instructed courses that last only five days. The graduating student earns a certification card that can be used to rent and buy gear and have tanks filled anywhere in the world.

Snorkeling. Although a great many visitors enjoy scuba diving in Hawaii, a great many more people see the underwater world with only mask, snorkel, and fins. If you are diving on your own, decide whether you or others traveling with you will be snorkeling, scuba diving, or mixing the two; then choose the dive site in this book accordingly. For instance, don't choose a spot that is indicated as being good only for scuba if there are snorkelers in your group. It is easy enough to choose a spot where both can enjoy the water.

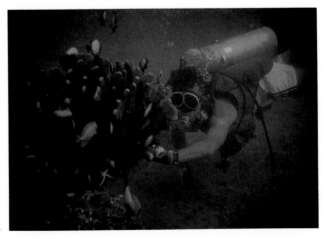

At Wailea Beach, a lone colony of coral crowns a coral boulder.

Tour Companies

If you go on an organized tour, choose the company with the same consideration. There are many different sorts of tours that are generally available.

Equipment Rental Companies. In well-developed areas, such as Honolulu and Waikiki on Oahu, Lahaina, Kaanapali, and Kihei on Maui, Kona on Hawaii, and Poipu and Kapaa on Kauai, a myriad of companies rent all kinds of gear from mopeds to surfboards to snorkeling gear and underwater cameras. These outfits generally don't rent scuba equipment. Furthermore, they only rent the gear, and you must supply your own transportation to and from the dive site.

Shuttle Companies. Shuttle companies rent snorkeling gear and offer transportation service to and from selected dive sites, primarily those sites on the extremely popular Hanauma Bay on Oahu. Most of these companies rent only snorkel gear and underwater cameras. They do not supply any sort of diving instruction or underwater guided tours; they merely rent you the gear, pick you up, and drop you off.

Dive Shops and Tour Companies. These generally offer both snorkeling and scuba diving. Often, however, these two activities are separate, and you must join either a skin or scuba group.

Big Boats. Some companies, particularly those running their trips on large boats, offer a mixture of snorkeling and scuba tours. This is the ideal for families and groups of people who have varied water interests. Waikiki, Lahaina, Kaanapali, Kihei, and Kona feature numerous large catamaran sailing vessels that visit the most beautiful beaches and reefs in the islands. Many of them offer scuba diving along with snorkeling, swimming, beachcombing, and sunbathing.

A dive boat anchors in the protected arms of Oahu's Hanauma Bay.

The V-striped butterfly fish is one of a seemingly endless variety of butterfly species found in Hawaii.

Diving Tips

A. When boat diving, always dive upcurrent. At the end of the dive you can ride the current back and avoid fatigue.

B. If you don't know what it is, don't touch it!

C. Stay clear of the black-and-white banded sea urchins.

D. If you are preparing to dive a site on your own but are unsure about conditions that day, or if you are uncertain about the correct place to enter and exit, call a dive shop, ask a life guard, or check with local experienced divers.

Fish and Game Regulations. You should be aware of some regulations established by the Division of Fish and Game concerning the collecting of various types of marine life.

1) Octopus less than 1 pound (2.2 kilograms) may not be taken.

2) Spiny and slipper lobsters may be taken only from September to May 1, and they must weigh more than 1 pound (2.2 kilograms). Females with eggs can't be collected, nor may you use a spear.

3) Collecting tropical fish for aquarium use requires a special license. No license is required for sportfishing, and the season is open all year.

4) No collecting of any kind is allowed in prescribed marine parks and sanctuaries. Such areas are well marked by signs.

5) No taking of live corals is allowed in less than 30 feet (10 meters) of water and within 1000 feet (300 meters) from shore.

More complete details on these and other regulations can be obtained from the local Division of Fish and Game office.

3

Diving in Oahu

Oahu contains the greatest abundance of diver-oriented services and facilities in the state. Equipment rentals and air fills are easily available all around the island, and there are many charter companies that specialize in underwater guided tours. The majority of shops and dive facilities are concentrated in the Honolulu and Waikiki areas, with other in Hawaii Kai, Kailua, Kaneohe, Aiea, Makaha, and Haleiwa.

Oahu's sheltered leeward coastline, which extends from Kaena Point to Diamond Head, is perhaps the most popular overall diving area because of its nearly year-round accessibility. In the tradewind shadow of the Waianae and Koolau mountains, waters tend to be calmer. The coastline from Barber's Point to Kaena Point is nearly uninterrupted beaches. Dives can be made almost anywhere along the way, but you have to nit the right places to find any reefs.

Extending from Diamond Head to Makapuu Point is a craggy, panoramic coastline characterized by sheer sea cliffs and often-pounding surf. This area also feels the grip of a treacherous current known as the Molokai Express. Slow-moving ocean currents funnel between Molokai and Oahu and result in a venturi effect that speeds water movement to as much as five knots. The Molokai Express is weakest near shore, so stay in close when diving this area.

On this side of Oahu you'll also find Hanauma Bay, one of the most scenic spots in all the islands. The remains of an ancient volcanic crater now open to the sea at one side, secluded Hanauma Bay is the perfect spot for seasoned and novice divers alike. There is a shallow inner reef for swimming and snorkeling and an out bay that offers deeper, clearer waters.

The windward side extends from Makapuu Point to Kahuku. Diving conditions are excellent during Kona weather on the offshore reefs. This side of Oahu, however, is generally under the influence of the normal tradewinds, and the water is too rough for diving most of the year.

The north shore of Oahu is a ribbon of wide sandy beaches adorned by inland coves and bays. During the summer months the high surf is on vacation and the area becomes a diver's paradise. It is a good area for the beginner.

Oahu, with the city of Honolulu and the beach at Waikiki, is the center of population and ▶ tourism in Hawaii. Development and good diving co-exist at many points around the island.

DIVE SITE RATINGS

Oahu

	Novice Diver	Novice w/instructor or divemaster	Intermediate Diver	Intermediate w/instructor or divemaster	Advanced Diver	Advanced w/instructor or divemaster
1 Leeward Wrecks: Maui and Seaplane			×	×	×	×
2 Kahe Point Beach Park (novice in shore)					×	×
3 Rainbow Reef	×	×	×	×	×	×
4 Magic Island			×	×	×	×
5 Hanauma Bay (novice on inner reef)			×	×	×	×
6 Blowhole			×	×	×	×
7 Rabbit Island and Makapuu Point					×	×
8 Shark's Cove	×	×	×	×	×	×
9 Three Tables			×	×	×	×
10 Waimea Bay	×	×	×	×	×	×

When using the accompanying chart see the information on page 5 for an explanation of the diver rating system and site locations

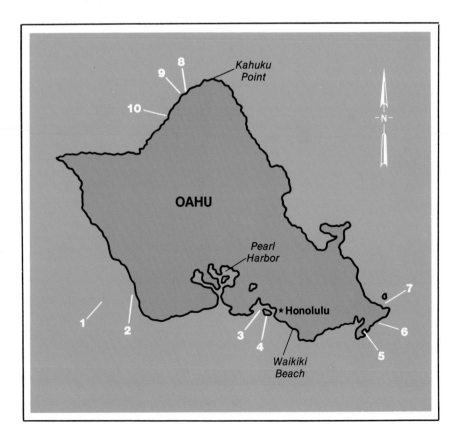

Typical depth range	:	90 feet (28 meters) to the bottom; about 60 feet (18 meters) on the top of the boat
Typical current conditions	:	Mild to non-existent during normal weather
Expertise required	:	Intermediate to advanced
Access	:	Boat

The waters around the Hawaiian Islands contain a number of sunken wrecks which have become artificial reefs—ships, planes, submarines, and other manmade products which have sunk in shallow water to become the home for a myriad of colorful and fascinating marine creatures. Most of these artificial reefs are the result of accidents: derelict remains of World War II, maritime mishaps, or the sometimes violent moods of weather in the sub-tropical Pacific Ocean.

In 1982 the first planned artificial reef was created: the M/V *Mahi*. The *Mahi* was originally built for the Navy, a 165 foot (50 meter), 600 ton vessel. It was later converted to an oceanographic research ship used by the University of Hawaii. No longer seaworthy, it was due to be sunk off Honolulu in deep water. Ken Taylor, owner and operator of South Seas Aquatics dive shop in Honolulu, intervened and with the help of local

The Mahi wreck, the state's first planned artificial reef, has become a popular residence for many reef creatures. Multi-hued encrusting sponges have begun to cover the hulk and rays and sea turtles have been seen nearby.

The plane, about 20 minutes away from the Mahi, is one of the most accessible airplane wrecks in the state.

volunteers had the plans changed so that the *Mahi* was sunk in shallow water as Hawaii's first planned artificial reef.

The *Mahi* is now one of the best, and certainly most accessible intact sunken wrecks in the state. It is located about a mile (1½ kilometers) offshore of Maile point and is visited by several dive tours, primarily those of South Seas Aquatics.

Airplane Wreck

About 20 minutes away from the *Mahi*, between Maile Point and Campbell Industrial Park, is another interesting sunken wreck, a plane. Approximately the same distance offshore as the *Mahi*, the plane lies in similar waters at depth of about 75 feet (23 meters). The propeller is still attached to the fuselage, and you can swim inside and sit in the pilot's seat the gauges and instrument panel are still there. If you're into wreck diving, don't miss these two.

Typical depth range	:	20–30 feet (6–10 meters)
Typical current conditions	:	Mild to non-existent while in the wind shadow; except Kona weather
Expertise required	:	Beginner near shore, advanced farther out near ledge
Access	:	Beach

The Kahe Point Beach Park is found at about 89-620 Farrington Highway 90, the entrance is marked by a sign on the highway, and it is an excellent spot for a family or group outing with swimming and snorkeling as well as scuba diving in calm, shallow water relatively near to shore.

Diving is not good off the beach park itself, as the bottom is mostly sand. The best spot to enter and exit is to the east of the beach (left side of the parking lot as you face the water) from a small rocky cove.

The bottom slopes very gently out from shore and for a long way is only about 20 feet (6 meters) deep. Near shore the bottom is mostly sand and large coral heads, but this develops into a lush coral reef further offshore. This is, in fact, one of the most extensive coral reefs on Oahu, and because it is in shallow water it is great for less experienced skin and scuba enthusiasts.

Underwater Scenery. For the first several dozen yards, or so you will see mostly sand, and visibility tends to be rather poor. Beyond this point are coral patches separated by sand, and good visibility as you reach

The goatfish is a cleaner—it removes and eats parasites from the skin of other fishes.

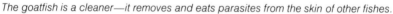

Known for its abundance of sea turtles, Kahe Point features patches of corals on a white sand bottom at depths of 20 to 30 feet (6-10 meters).

the coral reefs. Beginners and intermediate divers should stay within 200 yards (185 meters) of shore to keep within the protective wind shadow, but the experienced diver may wish to travel farther offshore. Some 400 yards (370 meters) out the depth is around 60 feet (18 meters) and visibility usually 100 feet (30 meters) or more. Out here you will find an interesting offshore ledge pock-marked with small grottos which are home to many fish and other smaller marine life forms. The area is also known among local divers for its abundance of turtles. Sharks are also sometimes sighted here.

Caution. If you do venture this far out, *be certain to leave sufficient air* for a return trip underwater to within the wind shadow before you have to surface.

Typical depth range	:	15–30 feet (5–10 meters) near shore, progressively deeper farther offshore
Typical current conditions	:	Mild to non-existent near shore most of the year
Expertise required	:	Novice to intermediate
Access	:	Beach

Like Kahe Point, this site makes an excellent family outing. Unlike Kahe, however, it cannot be reached from the shore, but only by boat. The area is visited daily by Dan's Dive Shop aboard a spacious sailing catamaran. The nice thing about the trip as a family outing is the variety: a pleasant sailboat ride to the reef with scenic Diamond Head in the background, anchoring on a picturesque coral reef, scuba diving, snorkeling, swimming, or just plain old loafing in the sun. Lunch and drinks are served, and the trip ends a sailing ride back to port.

The live coral and semi-tame tropical fish on Rainbow Reef make it an excellent site for underwater photography.

This catamaran makes the trip to Rainbow Reef daily. Good for snorkelers or divers, the boat trip also includes lunch, drinks and a sailing excursion.

Rainbow Reef itself makes for interesting underwater exploration. Located in very sheltered waters, it is an excellent spot for the less experienced snorkeler and scuba diver. For novices, skin and scuba instruction are provided, along with an underwater guided tour by professionals to make for a safe and enjoyable journey. One of the fun aspects of this spot is that the fish are accustomed to divers dropping in on them every day. The divers bring bread supplied by the boat and the fish have become quite friendly to say the least. The depth is shallow, anywhere from about 15 feet (5 meters) nearer shore to 30 feet (10 meters) or so farther out. Since the spot is located just beyond the surf line, it is well protected and waters generally are quite calm. The area offers a particularly nice live coral reef, which makes for fascinating exploration.

Underwater Photography. This is a scenic spot where rock and coral structures form a series of finger reefs running vertically offshore, with sand passageways in between. There is a good abundance of tropical fish that seem to have congregated here knowing that friendly divers bring them food daily. Because of the coral, the fish life, and the interesting terrain, Rainbow Reef is a very good spot to do some underwater photography. In fact, one of the unusual services offered by Dan's Dive Shop is its underwater photography service.

The trip to Rainbow Reef is one of the best bargains in Hawaiian diving and sightseeing, and it is highly recommended to both the novice and experienced skin and scuba diver. It's a great way to spend the day!

Typical depth range	:	20–50 feet (6–15 meters)
Typical current conditions	:	Some near-shore surge, but little current except during Kona weather
Expertise required	:	Intermediate to advanced
Access	:	Beach

A lovely sheltered beach and swimming area of Ala Moana Beach Park, adjacent to this site, lets non-divers enjoy themselves while the old salts explore the underwater world.

Entry and exit is most convenient from the right-hand side of the sea wall. Extreme caution must be used, however, as the wave-washed rocks tend to be slippery. Within the first 100 yards (90 meters) of shore the depth averages 20–30 feet (6–10 meters), with a visibility averaging 40–50 feet (12–15 meters). The bottom terrain is mostly hard rock, with small

The protection offered by its thick, strong spines allows the red slate-urchin to remain out in the open during the day, when many small reef creatures are hiding from predators.

Bigeyes are found throughout Hawaiian waters. Sometimes they are seen in great schools near shore. This delights Hawaiians in one respect because the fish are good to eat, but the schooling fish are said to portend the death of a high chief. Photo: B. Sastre.

caves found running between the many surge channels. A little further offshore the visibility improves, and at a depth of 50 feet (15 meters) sand and coral formations predominate.

Admittedly, Magic Island is not the best dive site on Oahu. However, it is very easily reached, just a short distance from Waikiki in Honolulu. Ala Moana Beach Park is perhaps the nicest beach park on Oahu, and right across the street from Ala Moana shopping center. Magic Island is a popular dive site with visitors because of its overall convenience: close to town with excellent facilities, yet offering some nice underwater sights as well. It's perfect for the more casual diver with family or friends who do not wish to visit more remote dive sites or spend the day waiting for the divers to get out of the water. At Magic Island and Ala Moana there is literally something for everyone.

Typical depth range	:	10 feet (3 meters) on the inner reef, sloping to 70 feet (23 meters) at the mouth of the bay
Typical current conditions	:	Generally non-existent
Expertise required	:	Novice on the inner reef, intermediate to advanced on the outer reef
Access	:	Beach

Hanauma Bay is one of the most beautiful spots in all the tropical Pacific. It is one of those panoramic extravanganzas of nature which must be seen to be believed. If you do nothing else on Oahu, visit Hanauma Bay. Even if you only peer over the scenic lookout (you won't be able to take your eyes away for some time), the sight will make your day.

Hanauma Bay is today one of the most sheltered in the state. Only when oddball winds blow up out of the southeast (only a few days a year) is the water rough and poor for diving. Most of the time it is ideal for family and group outings. Because it is such a popular spot, a large number of dive tour and shuttle companies run several trips daily to the bay from Waikiki.

Hanauma Bay is the very picture of a tropical Pacific lagoon. The inner reef—the dark patch of rocks and coral in the foreground—is excellent for novices and snorkelers. Due to wave action and swimmers, however, the visibility in this area is sometimes limited. The outer reef, at the mouth of the bay, provides greater visibility and a wider variety of marine life to experienced divers.

The Inner Reef. There are two diving areas within the bay. The first is the inner reef, which is like a giant swimming pool where the waters are almost always calm. Swimming is excellent here and in the several large pools within the reef itself. The maximum depth of the inner reef is 10 feet (3 meters), but most places are much shallower. Visibility tends to be poor depending on the daily conditions of water movement and or how many people are kicking about the stirring up the bottom sand. There is little coral in this area, but the volcanic rock topography is nice. Fish here are very tame because all of Hanauma Bay is a protected marine park. The inner reef is ideal for the beginning skin and scuba diver.

The Outer Reef. For the more experienced snorkeler and scuba enthusiast, the outer reef is a veritable underwater playground. The outer reef slopes gradually from 15 feet (5 meters) to around 70 feet (21 meters) near the mouth of the bay. Literally all areas of the bay, from just outside the inner barrier reef to the mouth of the bay are filled with lush coral gardens, an abundance of fish, turtles, and other interesting creatures.

For exploring just outside the inner reef and part-way out into the bay, intermediate skills are recommended. Only advanced divers should venture far out into the bay and to the mouth. This area does have some beautiful diving, but the water is deeper, currents begin to develop, and you will be quite a way from shore for the return swim.

A soldierfish nestles in the hollow of a rock coated with encrusting sponge on the outer reef at Hanauma Bay.

The Slot. To leave the inner reef and reach the outer bay, do not try and swim over the barrier reef. This is dangerous due to waves washing across the surface rocks. There is a passage through the reef, known to local divers as "the slot," which makes a convenient entry and exit point to and from the inner reef. To find the slot, you should walk to the right along the beach past the snack bar to the lifeguard stand. Just about straight out from that point is the slot, and to help you spot it before you get in the water, ask the lifeguard to point it out to you. A large diameter cable runs through this channel and can be followed a good distance out into the bay, and it can be used to indicate the way back through the slot at the completion of the dive. The outer bay can also be entered from either side along the perimeter by walking, but is not as convenient or safe as swimming out from the inner reef area.

Witch's Brew. Although the bay offers good diving everywhere, there is a particular interesting area on the right-hand side close to shore. To the right, out along the crescent arm of the crater wall, is a small peninsula that juts out from shore. In front of this peninsula is a lush coral reef and huge surge channels that make for some exciting diving and scenic topography. This area is known as Witch's Brew because several different wave and current patterns merge at this point. The result is turbulent surface waters and back-and-forth surging currents on the bottom down to about 30 feet (10 meters). Most of the time the currents are not severe, but they do tend to move you around and care must be exercised not to get scraped across the sharp coral.

Underwater Photography. Hanuama Bay is one of the best spots in all the state to get some really nice underwater photos. The clear water and varied seascapes produce excellent diver scenics, while the plentiful and friendly fish offer the best in close-up picture taking.

A diver cautiously touches a red slate-pencil urchin. Unlike the long-spine urchin, whose quills can penetrate even thick gloves, the slate-pencil urchin's spines are not dangerous.

Typical depth range	:	20–60 feet (6–18 meters)
Typical current condition	:	Generally little current within 100 yards (90 meters) of shore, "Molokai Express" further out
Expertise required	:	Intermediate to advanced
Access	:	Beach

A secluded beach little known to visitors but popular among locals is the cove near the Blowhole lookout. If you take the coastal Kalanianaole Highway 72 past Hanauma Bay you will be coming on a sign indicating the Blowhole lookout. Park in this area. There are no public facilities, but the beach is nice for sunbathing before or after the dive. Much of the year the surf is mild and you can follow the underwater corridor out of the cove into some interesting diving.

The area is characterized by patches of rock and coral with sand stretches in between. Visibility is poor close to shore due to wave action, but the bottom slopes gently from about 15 feet (5 meters) at the mouth of the cove, and farther offshore in deeper water visibility becomes much better. The best diving is found to the right as you swim outside the cove. It becomes much deeper at a much greater rate here than it does going straight out of or to the left of the cove. This deeper area to the right features some fascinating ledges and cliffs, one of which drops straight down from 20 to 60 feet (6 to 18 meters).

A shy pufferfish prepares to dart into a hole in the reef to escape the attentions of an underwater photographer.

In the deeper area at the Blowhole, a ledge drops from 20 to 60 feet (6 to 18 meters), framing a diver against the bright, subtropical sun.

Although the small beach affords safe entry and exit, care should be taken when going through the waves because there are rocks. Remember the Molokai Express—it can be a treacherous, unforgiving current if you venture too far offshore. Stay within 100 yards (90 meters) of the shore, and to be on the safe side, try and dive Blowhole only at slack or incoming tide.

Typical depth range	:	50–60 feet (15–18 meters)
Typical current condition	:	Can be swift and require caution
Expertise required	:	Advanced
Access	:	Boat

Continuing on the coastline road from Blowhole, you come up the panoramic splendor of Makapuu Beach and offshore Rabbit Island.

The underwater terrain between the island and Makapuu Beach is quite interesting. Although the hardy diver might be tempted to swim to the island from the beach, don't try it. Stick with a boat dive. Wave and current action can be strong here, and sharks are frequently spotted in this open ocean habitat. The depth runs anywhere around 50 to 60 feet (15–18 meters) with variable visibility that is often quite good. The bottom is mostly basalt lava rock with a lot of coral growth and not much sand.

Rubble-like piles of volcanic rock and coral line the bottom between Rabbit Island and Makapuu Beach.

Between Rabbit Island (left) and its flat neighbor, a patch reef of varied corals can be found in just 35 feet (11 meters) of water.

Unusual Reef Life. A particularly interesting spot is between Rabbit Island and its small nearby neighbor, low-lying Kaohikaipu (don't bother trying to pronounce it!) Island. Here you will find a lovely coral reef in only 35 feet (11 meters) of water. In this open ocean environment, you can expect to see fewer small tropical fish and more of larger pelagic life forms, such as large schools of fish, turtles, ulua, and even sharks.

Typical depth range	:	20–50 feet (6–15 meters) near shore, sloping gradually deeper
Typical current condition	:	Hazardous during winter, generally calm during summer
Expertise required	:	Novice to intermediate
Access	:	Beach

Also referred to as Pupukea, Shark's Cove is perhaps the most popular of all north shore dive sites. During the summer months from May to October it is almost always calm with little if any current or wave action. It is thus an excellent spot for beginning divers to sharpen their underwater skills. It is also popular with more advanced divers because of the labyrinthine network of undersea caves and caverns.

Shark's Cove was not named for the presence of its toothy namesake, but because some imaginative diver thought certain of the rocks there resembled a shark.

Actually, good diving is not to be found within the cove itself, but outside it. Entry and exit from the water, however, are most conveniently accomplished from the sandy beaches that ring the cove. After a brief swim of less than 100 feet (30 meters) is the cave mouth in about 20 feet (6 meters) of water. Visibility is poor in the cove but improves immediately outside.

One entrance to the underwater caves at Shark's Cove can be found in the shoreline reef to the right of the cove. The best way to reach the caves, however, is by entering the water at the beach and swimming through the mouth of the cove.

Numerous caves undercut the volcanic rock shore at Sharks Cove. Though many are only 20 to 30 feet long and open to the sea on both ends, novices should go no further than the mouth of these tunnels.

Underwater Terrain. Approximately 100 yards (90 meters) past the mouth of Shark's Cove you will come on caverns of varying sizes carved under the volcanic rock shoreline. The great majority of caves and passageways run but a few dozen feet (about 8–12 meters) before opening out into the blue water again, and make for fascinating exploration. Some caves, on the other hand, especially those found farther down along the coastline, penetrate deep back into the rock. These should be reserved only for the experienced and knowledgeable cave diver, and you should never penetrate so deeply as to lose sight of the entrance. Also, when entering a cavern, remember that the water will be clear at first, but as you penetrate further sand and silt tend to be stirred up by kicking fins and bubble exhalations, and the entrance can be quickly obscured. Caution is the watchword when entering any underwater cave, no matter how shallow it may be. Novice divers should not penetrate deeper than just inside a cave entrance unless accompanied by a professional tour guide or instructor. Additionally, even if you are an advanced diver, you should check the surge conditions that day. Before entering a cave, swim around outside for a few minutes to see how the surge currents are behaving. During the summer months most days will be calm, but on some days there will be strong water surges that can throw you helplessly about inside a cave if you are not extremely careful.

The delicate tendrils of a coral polyp spreading out to filter food is one of the sights that enhance night diving at Shark's Cove.

Night Diving. If you are a night diver, Shark's Cove is a great spot to visit during the summer months. The best way to dive this area at night is to swim out and find the dive site just before sundown. For night diving you are best off going to the left of the cove. There are no caves there but a much greater abundance of marine life for after-dark sightseeing. This is a particularly good area for underwater photography at night, the black background water producing an excellent contrast to the bright yellow coral polyps, flame orange crabs, multi-colored nudibranchs and sea shells, big-eyed squirrelfish, and much more.

Night diving at Shark's Cove is recommended only for the advanced diver experienced in the exploration of the water world after dark. Near shore the depths do not exceed 50 feet (15 meters), and it is important not to lose track of the mouth of the cove which is the only good place to exit from the water, the rest of the surrounding coastline being rugged wave-washed lava rock.

Before attempting a night dive at Shark's Cove it is best to check recent weather and water conditions with a dive shop, and weather for the night with the weather service. Only dive the area at night if the surf is down, the weather is good, and the water in the cove is calm. With a little caution, a night dive at Shark's Cove can be one of the highlights of your Hawaiian diving.

Parrotfish, gregarious and active during the day, back themselves into protective cubbyholes during the night. After bedding down, they surround themselves with a secretion which forms a thin, translucent bubble.

Typical depth range	:	20–60 feet (6–18 meters)
Typical current conditions	:	Hazardous during winter, generally calm during summer
Expertise required	:	Intermediate to advanced
Access	:	Beach

Three Tables is less than a mile (1½ kilometers) down the road from Shark's Cove on the way to Waimea beach on Kamehameha Highway 83. Three Tables is a superior dive site to Waimea in terms of underwater terrain and marine life, but it requires a slightly higher skill level.

Three Tables is so named because of offshore ledges which produce really spectacular seascapes featuring arches, overhangs, and large crevasses to explore. The best entry and exit points are along the rocky shoreline in front of the parking area. This shoreline does require caution, however, when getting in and out of the water due to wave action. Visibility tends to be rather poor near shore but gets steadily better the further out you swim. The bottom is very rocky, sloping gently outward.

A diver feeds a spotted eel during a night dive. Even heavy gloves are no match for the eel's sharp teeth, and the small creatures can unintentionally slice up a finger while feeding.

Another colorful reef inhabitant active at night is the lobster. A relative of the larger—and somewhat tastier—Maine lobster, this species lacks the crusher claw.

Near shore the depths runs around 20–30 feet (6–10 meters), and the area is characterized by large pot-hole depressions in the rock substrate with many interconnecting tunnels and passageways.

The best locations for diving are not straight offshore but to the right, found by swimming out diagonally about half the distance to Shark's Cove. It's a fairly long swim of 15 to 20 minutes and is best done on the surface, snorkeling to conserve air. At a distance of 100 to 200 yards (90–180 meters) offshore the water is the clearest, with a depth averaging 60 feet (18 meters). It's a great lobster area because of the caverns, lava tubes, huge overhangs, and the like. Large Conger eels are frequently spotted here, along with a varied marine population of fish, nudibranchs, crustaceans, and so on.

Typical depth range	:	10–30 feet (3–10 meters)
Typical current conditions	:	Dangerous surf and currents during winter months, generally calm during summer
Expertise required	:	Novice
Access	:	Beach

After Hanauma Bay, Waimea may be the most picturesque beach on Oahu, certainly on the north shore. Even if you are a two-tank diver and make your two dives at Shark's Cove and Three Tables, Waimea is a great place to finish the day with a picnic and relaxation.

Good Novice Diving. Waimea is not recommended for the intermediate and advanced diver simply because it doesn't offer the underwater scenery and marine life that nearby Three Tables and Shark's Cove do. Waimea, on the other hand, is highly recommended for the novice diver who wishes to log some bottom time in calm, easily diveable waters. The spot to go is on the left-hand side of the bay, out around the big rocks. This

The large eyes of the squirrelfish mark it as another nocturnal creature. During the day, they can sometimes be found in shady recesses under reefs or rocks.

The rocks at left are the best dive site at Waimea Bay. The bay is calm and a good site for beginners. More experienced divers may appreciate the beach, which is one of the state's most scenic.

area is very near to shore, requiring but a short, easy swim. Near shore the water surge may or may not throw you around a bit, depending on the day. The visibility is normally not the best in so close with the depth being only 10 or 15 feet (3–5 meters). A little further offshore, but still within a few hundred feet (60–90 meters), the depth gets to be 20 feet (6 meters) or more and visibility improves.

Underwater Scenery and Marine Life. The area is strewn with large volcanic boulders ranging anywhere from less than a foot (30 centimeters) to many feet in size, with some large ones being 10 feet (3 meters) and more. There is little coral growth on the rocks; the rest of the area is sand which slopes gradually outward from the beach. The marine life consists of small tropical fish but not a lot of other growth, because during the winter months huge surf up to 40 feet (12 meters) high pounds the rocks. Waimea is an excellent novice snorkeling place; again, not so much for the scenery but because it is such a calm, easy spot to dive. Great for kids and other folks who may not be comfortable in the water, yet would still like to see something of the underwater world.

4

Diving in Maui

Maui offers top-notch dive shops and underwater tour companies in Kaanapali, Lahaina, and Kihei/Wailea. The longest coastline on Maui is the north shore, but it is infrequently dived because of its remoteness and the year-round rough waters. The windward southeast shore is also generally off limits because of winds, swells, and currents.

Maui's leeward shore, from La Perouse to Kaanapali, has the best diving. Every hotel on or near the beach has a beach activities operation which provides every service from renting dive gear, to teaching snorkeling and scuba diving, to signing you up for boat trips to nearby islands.

Actually, some of the better diving is not found on Maui proper but on the nearby islet of Molokini and the south shore of Lanai. Three dive sites for these islands are also covered in this chapter.

From November to April, you might be able to catch one of the biggest thrills in Maui's marine world: the possibility of seeing first-hand the mammoth humpback whales which migrate to Hawaii each year. Even if you don't catch a glimpse of them, you'll know the gentle giants are nearby; once underwater you can hear their pleasant song echoing as they communicate with one another.

With a variety of hotel and beachfront dive operations to choose from, Maui offers very convenient diving both around the island and at nearby Molokini Crater and Lanai. ▶

DIVE SITE RATINGS

Maui

	Novice Diver	Novice w/instructor or divemaster	Intermediate Diver	Intermediate w/instructor or divemaster	Advanced Diver	Advanced w/instructor or divemaster
1 Molokini Crater (novice in shallow water)					×	×
2 Lanai Island—Hulapoe Bay*	×	×	×	×	×	×
3 Lanai Island—the Cathedrals					×	×
4 Honolua Bay	×	×	×	×	×	×
5 Black Rock* (novice inside sheltered cove)			×	×	×	×
6 Olowalu*	×	×	×	×	×	×
7 Wailea Beach* (novice inshore)			×	×	×	×
8 Cemetery or Five Coves*			×	×	×	×
9 Makena Beach*			×	×	×	×
10 Hana Bay*			×	×	×	×

*Indicates good snorkeling spot.

When using the accompanying chart see the information on page 5 for an explanation of the diver rating system and site locations.

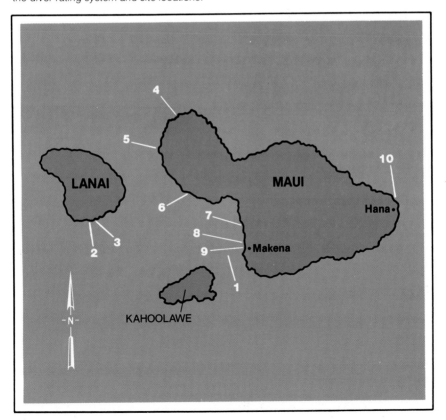

Typical depth range	:	10 feet (3 meters) near shore to about 60–90 feet (18–27 meters) feet at the drop-off
Typical current conditions	:	Mild or non-existent during the morning, strong in afternoon
Expertise required	:	Novice in shallow nearshore waters to advanced in deep water and over the drop-off
Access	:	Boat

Molokini is a small islet, actually the tip of a small extinct volcanic crater barely one quarter (400 meters) in length, rising out of the blue between Maui and Kahoolawe. One half of the crater is still intact above water, the other half having long since been eroded away. Molokini is 45 minutes to an hour away by boat. The attractions: a panoramic view which takes in no less than 5 of the 8 major Hawaiian Islands; majestic coral formations; spectacular walls and drop-offs; whale and porpoise watching; and hand-feeding schools of tame tropical fish. This dive spot comes highly recommended!

Both snorkeling and scuba are terrific at Molokini. Snorkelers generally find the shallow, inner near-shore crater waters more calm and thus best for surface swimming. Depth here ranges anywhere from 10 to 30 feet (3–10 meters) the bottom sloping down gradually to 60–90 feet (18–27 meters) near the ledges. Scuba diving boats frequently anchor to the left side opposite the lighthouse, where the bottom terrain goes from a barrier reef submerged less than 10 feet (3 meters) to a breathtaking drop-off that plummets to waters over 200 feet (60 meters) deep.

The swarms of tropical fish within the crater are friendly to say the least. They are long accustomed to having visiting divers drop in on them with handfuls of bread, so be prepared to be swarmed by hundreds of small, curious yellow butterfly fish which will crowd about to be hand fed.

A wide variety of charter boats trek daily to Molokini (weather conditions permitting), carrying sightseers and skin and scuba divers from Wailea, Kihei, Maalaea Bay, and Lahaina. Morning is the best time to experience Molokini; the waters tend to be calmer, while during the afternoon wind and waves pick up and things can get pretty rough.

If you do no other diving in Maui, don't miss Molokini.

A protected marine park, Molokini Crater, the remnants of a volcano, is exciting for snorkelers and divers. Hordes of tropical fish, such as the lemon butterfly fish in the foreground, can be attracted by bringing a little food along. ▶

Typical depth range	:	10– 30 feet (3–10 meters)
Typical current conditions	:	Non-existent within the bay
Expertise required	:	Novice
Access	:	Beach

Maui's nearby neighbor is Lanai, also known as the "Pineapple Island." The entire island is owned by the Dole Corporation, and the industry there, as might be expected, is pineapple growing. It is a rural island with a population of only 2000. Lanai City does contain a small countryish inn, and there are some rental vehicles and ground tours available for those who are interested.

An Underwater Park. The residents of Lanai some years ago began fighting, and finally won, a battle to have beautiful Hulopoe Bay on the island's south shore officially sanctioned as an underwater park. The Island's best swimming bay is now protected from pollution, depletion of fish, and destruction of coral by divers and anchoring boats.

The visitor reaches Lanai by boat from Maui; it is a day-long affair. Incoming vessels are not permitted to anchor in Hulopoe Bay itself, but most off-load passengers at nearby Manele Harbor. A 15 minute walk brings you to the idyllic South Seas beauty of Hulopoe Bay.

Snorkeling. Hulopoe is visited daily by large sailing and motor vessels. These generally allow only snorkeling, not scuba, and are planned more as family and group outings with a shoreside barbeque and open bar on the return trip.

The most interesting part of the bay is on the left-hand side. There is a wide reef ledge with large tide pools for interesting exploration and swimming. Just over this ledge is a shallow submerged reef teeming with schools of bright tropical fish, and turtles are occasionally seen leisurely finning by. It's an excellent spot for the novice snorkeler, since complete instruction is provided in the calm, bathtub-warm waters of Hulopoe.

Although dive boats come into Hulopoe, the main scuba interest in Lanai is the nearby Cathedrals.

Like Molokini Crater, Hulopoe Bay on the shore of Lanai Island is a marine park. Dive and snorkel boats, which make the run to Holopoe Bay from Maui, can be seen in the background.

Typical depth range   :   70 feet (21 meters)
Typical current conditions :   Mild to treacherous
Expertise required   :   Advanced
Access   :   Boat

Offshore from Hulopoe Bay are two of Lanai's standout dive sites—the Cathedrals. Located within a few miles (less than 5 kilometers) of each other, the first and second cathedrals are huge underwater grottos that form a series of lava arches, caverns, pinnacles, tubes, ridges, and interconnecting passageways. When the water is calm, the visibility is generally in excess of 100 feet (30 meters).

The Cathedrals on Lanai are large, dramatic underwater caves. Tortuous interconnecting lava tubes open into enormous caverns, dappled with sunlight streaming through crevices in the rocky ceilings.

Schools of moorish idols can be found in the recesses of the Cathedrals. Other tropical species abound, and eagle rays sometimes graze the sand channels between the cavern structures.

When you enter the mammoth undersea grottos, you soon see how the Cathedrals got their names. Narrow passageways open into caves which in turn open into vast cathedral-like chambers. Looking up, you see sunlight filtering in through holes in the rocky ceiling, producing fantastic light patterns that shimmer and dance laser-like in the darkened amphitheater. The sight is reminiscent of glass windows in a cathedral.

Unusual Marine Life. The area abounds in clouds of small tropical fish which seem to segregate themselves in according to color. Many specimens of delicately painted butterflyfish thrive here, there are schools of Moorish Idols, and within the nooks and crannies are lobsters, crabs, and other curious creatures.

Morning is the best time to dive the Cathedrals, when the wind and water swell is down. In the afternoon swift currents may develop unexpectedly, with tremendous water surges stirring up the bottom and reducing the visibility from 100 feet (30 meters) to zero. The Cathedrals should only be dived with experienced local dive tours.

Typical depth range	:	10–40 feet (3–12 meters)
Typical current conditions	:	Calm during the summer months, rough to undiveable in the winter
Expertise required	:	Novice to intermediate
Access	:	Beach

Located at the westernmost tip of Maui is Honolua Bay. Honolua and adjoining Makuleia Bay are found some 8 miles (13 kilometers) north of Kaanapali by following Route 30, the Honoapiilani highway.

Marine Life. Both sides of the bay feature lovely, well-developed coral reefs in shallow water of 40 feet (12 meters) and less. Between these reefs, in the center of the bay, is only a sandy bottom. The fish to be seen in the greatest numbers on the Honolua reefs are species of wrasse, primarily the saddleback variety with a blue head, a green tail, and a red midsection or "saddle." The Hawaiian name for these reef fish, common to all Hawaiian waters, is *hinalea*. Nature seems to have endowed these finned creatures with an unusual sense of curiousity. They are well-known for following divers about, darting in close to peer into a face mask to see what you are up to.

Though the corals of Hawaii are somewhat scrubby when compared with the best growth of the Caribbean and Micronesia, the beauty of the fish species is abundant compensation. The ornate butterfly fish is just one example.

Honolua Bay, on the western tip of Maui, is another protected marine park. Two reefs, on the two sides of the bay, are separated by a flat sand bottom.

There do not tend to be any large, spectacularly towering coral or rock formations, although there are a smattering of small caves along the left side of the bay. The coral growth is lush, however, and the marine life plentiful. Remember, Honolua Bay is a protected Marine Preserve, and the collection of shells, coral, and fish is strictly prohibited.

Geographically Honolua Bay is on the tip of west Maui just before the beginning of the north shore. At the north shore of any of the Hawaiian Islands, time of year and daily weather conditions are important factors to be considered before attempting to dive safely. Diving is best during the summer months or whenever the water is flat. The best time of day is in the morning, before the wind and waves come up. Honolua Bay also has an international reputation among surfers who flock here to compete during the winter months when the big surf rolls in. Do not attempt to dive the bay during such times!

Typical depth range	:	20 feet (6 meters) in the cove area
Typical current conditions	:	Non-existent most of the year
Expertise required	:	Novice inside the sheltered cove; intermediate outside
Access	:	Beach

Black Rock is probably the easiest, safest, and most convenient dive spot on Maui. It is located on Kaanapali beach, in front of the Sheraton Hotel. While the large expanse of Kaanapali beach consists of only sandy bottom terrain, a large black volcanic rock peninsula juts out several hundred feet from shore, providing a protected cove that is excellent for the novice snorkeler and scuba enthusiast. The hotels in the area, primarily the Sheraton and Kaanapali Beach Hotel, rent snorkel and scuba gear and underwater cameras; they also provide instruction.

The underwater terrain contains a little coral, but mostly volcanic rock, with an abundance of tame tropical fish. In places such as Black Rock and Molokini where divers drop into the water everyday, colorful reef fish have become extremely tame. They are used to being fed and swarm about scuba divers and snorkelers alike. Great for pictures!

Kaanapali Beach, viewed from the top of the Sheraton Hotel, is the site of the Black Rock diving area. The best diving is found in the area at the extreme right side of the photo.

The best entry is the beach adjoining the Black Rock peninsula. For the snorkeler who is not weighted down with cumbersome scuba gear, entry can also be made from the rock jetty itself, but watch out for ocean swell and waves. The sheltered inner cove is recommended for the novice skin and scuba diver. Those with more experience, will find better visibility and more marine life by swimming out around the rocky peninsula to the north. Depending on daily conditions though, there may be a bit of a current to contend with. The water tends to be clearer on the outside, and the rocky shoreline provides for some good scenery and fish life.

Although Black Rock is not the best beach dive to be found on Maui, at least in terms of scenic seascapes and abundance of coral and marine life, it does offer proximity, ease of diving, an excellent beach, and shoreside ammenities and services. It may be the best spot for those who wish to get a taste of the excitement of the underwater world without going through the time, expense, and trouble of a long boat ride or a drive to more distant dive sites. Black Rock is also highly recommended for beginning night divers.

Beginning night divers and snorkelers who don't want to spend all day on a boat find the marine life at Black Rock a good substitute for an excursion to Molokini.

Typical depth range	:	35 feet (11 meters) on the reefs to unlimited
Typical current conditions	:	Generally mild to non-existent
Expertise required	:	Novice
Access	:	Beach

Olowalu is one of the best sites for underwater scenery and marine life. Getting here does require a few more miles of driving, but the site is very accessible and an easily dived area for the beginner.

A freckled hawkfish caught in a characteristic pose, perched atop a small coral colony.

Easy entry, plentiful marine life and shallow water make Olowalu a good choice for snorkelers and divers willing to drive a little bit out of their way.

As you drive east from Lahaina, you will come to the Olowalu General Store. Go about a mile (1½ kilometers) further and you can dive nearly anywhere along the beachfront. There is a long stretch of sandy beach that makes for easy entry and exit. However, there are few shade trees at Olowalu, so things can get pretty uncomfortable.

Only when the surf is up is this area not good for diving. The coral is shallow and dangerous when the water's rough, and if you see surfers out on the water, you can assume good surfing conditions that are poor for diving, so try another spot for safety's sake.

When the surf is down, however, there is a lot to see. This area features good coral reef development and it is a good place for underwater photography—you will see an abundance of reef life. Nearer to shore the water is rather shallow and recommended for the snorkelers. It's really too shallow for scuba, and those with tanks should swim further out to deeper water. Although you will not see such spectacular underwater terrain as dramatic coral heads, lava tubes, and the like (the reef topography is flatter), this is an excellent spot for easily accessible reef diving by the neophyte snorkeler and scuba diver.

Typical depth range : 55 feet (17 meters)

Typical current conditions : Mild to non-existent most of the year

Expertise required : Novice near shore, intermediate further out and along the coastline

Access : Beach

Wailea Beach and the offshore reef extending south to Polo beach offer some of East Maui's easiest and nicest skin and scuba diving. To find the beach, travel toward Makena, past the Intercontinental Hotel and Wailea Shopping Village on your right, until you see the sign indicating Wailea Beach. There is a paved parking lot and you must walk a short distance

When alarmed or threatened by a predator, the porcupine fish assumes a most unappetizing appearance. By swallowing water, the fish expands its girth, causing the spines on its skin to stick straight out.

Potter's angelfish is one of the more brilliantly-colored of the angelfish family found in Hawaiian waters.

down to the water. Sticking straight out from shore is a large outcropping of lava rock which makes the best entry and exit points.

The best diving sites are out along this lava rock outcropping. The reef extends around the coastline and you can follow it all the way to Polo beach if you're a hardy swimmer. Keep in mind that skin and scuba divers not venturing too far from Wailea beach need only have beginning abilities, while swimming further out requires intermediate skills.

The reef is quite extensive with some very nice scenery, though without the abundance of fish life you will see elsewhere. The farther out you go, and the deeper, the more you can expect to see. If you plan to swim from Wailea to Polo beach to see all the sights along the way, it is recommended that you have someone drive the car to meet you at Polo beach—the last before you get to Makena where the road gets rough. Only attempt the swim if you're in good shape.

Typical depth range : 45–50 feet (14–15 meters)
Typical current conditions : Generally mild to non-existent
Expertise required : Intermediate
Access : Beach

If you're superstitious, the Cemetery may not be for you. About 1¼ miles (2 kilometers) past Polo beach toward Makena you come upon, what else, a cemetary; park here and walk down to the water. The surf can be a bit rough, depending on daily weather conditions, so check it out carefully before entering. If it's at all rough, it's safest to wait until another time.

Once in the water, swim straight out offshore until the water is about 40–45 feet (12–14 meters) deep. On the right-hand side of the submerged reef you will find a series of caves. This spot is locally referred to as the 5 caves (sometimes to the 5 graves because of the site's proximity the cemetary), but once underwater you'll forget such superstitions because the seascape terrain is quite scenic. Unlike previous Kihei dive sites which possess predominantly flat bottom terrain, this spot has some good relief and a lot of fish and marine life. Turtles are frequently sighted here, no doubt due to the better bottom relief and presence of underwater caves and caverns. Local divers also report a resident white-tip shark which lives in the Makena waters.

Sea turtles, which may hide in the caves and crevices of the reef, are often spotted at the Cemetery/Five Caves site near Makena.

Typical depth range	:	45 feet (14 meters)
Typical current conditions	:	Generally mild to non-existent
Expertise required	:	Intermediate
Access	:	Beach

Just as Maui is described as *no ka oi* (the best), Makena is certainly *no ka oi* among the beaches on this side of the island. Makena is about 3 miles (5 kilometers) past Polo beach along the Makena dirt road.

There are two dive spots on the right-hand side of the long crescent of Makena beach. The rocky coastline peninsula just to the right of the beach is the closest and easiest spot to dive. Swim to the right out along this peninsula to find the best skin and scuba diving.

The best diving at Makena requires a bit of a walk, but once at small beach you'll find probably the finest beach-access skin and scuba diving on this side of the island. The choicest spots are found by swimming out from the right side of this beach along the coastline. The underwater terrain features good topographic relief, caves, and an abundance of fish and marine life.

The fish found at Makena Beach are tame enough to feed by hand. A few breakfast scraps spread around in the water will soon attract a drove of bright tropical species.

Typical depth range	:	60 feet (18 meters)
Typical current conditions	:	Generally mild in the bay, but stronger near the mouth and outside
Expertise required	:	Intermediate to advanced
Access	:	Beach

Try a dive in Hana Bay. There is good diving on the very right-hand side out past the beach park and snack bar. This is not recommended for the novice diver, and much of the year should only be attempted by the more advanced diver. Hana Bay catches the gusty trades most of the year, and there is a 50/50 chance that diving here will be good and safe on any given day. You can get some idea of diveability ahead of time by calling the Marine forecaster before you leave for Hana. There are no dive facilities nearby, so you will have to rent your gear elsewhere and bring it with you.

There are two entry spots past the snack bar and opposite the wharf. There is a boat ramp on the inside of the pier, which is probably the easiest entry and exit point, but it requires a bit of a swim to get to the good diving out near the lighthouse. For those who wish to save the swim, there is a path way beyond the parking area that leads out toward the lighthouse for entry.

Parrotfish like this one are often seen on the reef "grazing" from one coral head to the next. Photo: B. Sastre.

Hana Bay, an area for more advanced divers, offers good coral development in the areas beyond the lighthouse. Snorkelers should not swim out past the lighthouse because the currents can be strong.

It is strongly recommended that snorkelers swim not out past the lighthouse, because surface waters become choppy and currents can be strong. For the scuba diver the best spot is beyond the lighthouse to the right, where you can expect to see beautiful coral, good bottom terrain, and fish life. Watch the currents!

5

Diving the Big Island of Hawaii

The Kona Coast of Hawaii offers what many people feel to be the best diving in the state. Maui's underwater enthusiasts may disagree, but only to an extent—Kona has some great diving! The southernmost island, Hawaii possesses the most extensive and well-developed coral reefs. The isle has 3 long coastlines, but due to water conditions only the leeward Kona side is regularly dived. The waters on the Hilo side, because they face directly into the breath of the trades, should not be dived except with a dive shop guide who knows the local waters. Dive sites are fairly inaccessible from shore; most require boat access and you have to know the right places to go at the right time for comfortable, safe diving. Some spots, such as Waipio Bay, are so scenic above water that you figure they must be terrific underwater as well, but unfortunately this is not always the case. If you want to dive the Hilo side, check with Nautilus Dive shop first.

The Kona coast is certainly the easiest side of the island to dive. Local divers, in fact, say it's hard to find a bad spot anywhere from Mahukona to South Point.

Sandy Beaches, and Bays that indent the coastline are an example of Hawaii's tropical charm.

DIVE SITE RATINGS

Hawaii

	Novice Diver	Novice w/instructor or divemaster	Intermediate Diver	Intermediate w/instructor or divemaster	Advanced Diver	Advanced w/instructor or divemaster
1 Puako/Mauna Kea Beach Hotel (novice for Boat Dives only)			×	×	×	×
2 Kona Surf Hotel	×	×	×	×	×	×
3 Honaunau Bay*	×	×	×	×	×	×
4 Red Hill	×	×	×	×	×	×
5 Kealakekua Bay*	×	×	×	×	×	×

*Indicates good snorkeling spot.

When using the accompanying chart see the information on page 5 for an explanation of the diver rating system and site locations

The long Kona Coast of the Big Island of Hawaii offers fine diving in the lee of the prevailing trade winds.

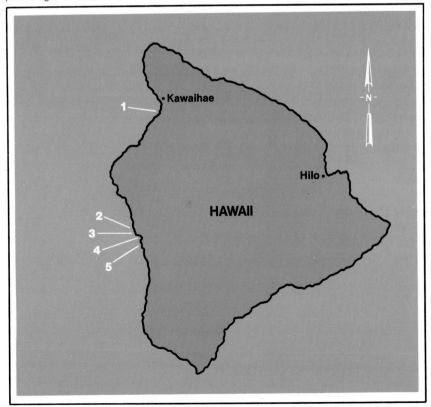

Typical depth range	:	20–90 feet (6–30 meters)
Typical current conditions	:	Negligible much of the year, but the surf can be unpredictable for shore dives
Expertise required	:	Novice to intermediate for boat dives, intermediate to advanced for shore dives
Access	:	Beach or boat

Puako offers many dive sites located along stretch of coastline good for boat dives, and others along a 2-mile (3 kilometer) stretch of the Puako beach road just off Highway 19 some 25 miles (40 kilometers) north of Kona.

A word of caution about shore diving: there is no beach, only sharp volcanic rock which you must cross to reach the water. Wear tennis shoes, or at least sandals, to save your feet. The waveswept rocks are also very slippery and dangerous. But perhaps the worst thing about shore diving Puako is the surf—it can be flat as a lake when you submerge, yet like a maelstrom when you surface, making exit hazardous. The best, calmest time to dive is morning. Almost assuredly the surf will be up in the afternoon.

Shore diving at Puako is well worth it once you're in the water. The reef edge drops to depths of about 15 to 20 feet (5–6 meters), gradually sloping out to 60–90 feet (18–30 meters) at the drop-off further offshore. The shoreline is cut by surge channels which produce fantastic topography including arch-like canyons, lava tubes, tunnels, walls, caverns, and the like. Within a few hundred feet offshore towering coral reef formations take over, with valleys and rises 20–30 feet (6–10 meters) high, a splendid seascape with endless terrain to explore. Schools of tropical fish abound. Turtles are frequently sighted and you may come upon them resting in the larger grottos. During the season, whales are often seen playing in the calm waters near shore.

If you like to dive on your own, Puako is a good spot if keep in mind the rigors of shore entry and the skill level required to dive safely. You can stay nearby at the Puako Beach Apartments. To get tanks rented and filled, check with Professional Divers Hawaii in Kawaihae.

Benefitting from the Big Island's position at the southernmost edge of the Hawaiian chain, Puako displays some of the most beautiful coral in the entire state. Turtles are often seen among the caves and undercuts in the reef and, in season, whales can be seen in the calm waters near shore. Orange coral like this can be seen in the reefs just offshore. Photo: B. Sastre.

Guided Tours. The best dive sites between Puako and Mahukona can be reached onboard the Mauna Kea Beach Hotel's 58-foot (18-meter) sailing catamaran. The boat loads each morning at 9:00 A.M. from the beach in front of the hotel.

The coastline further north is similar to Puako, and the boat anchors in sheltered areas with good visibility, excellent underwater topography, and lots of marine life. Underwater cameras are also available. A lot of dive sites in the Mahukona area feature caves and tunnels which penetrate back under the shoreline, with lobster seen on most dives.

After a day of diving off the boat, the sailing trip back to the hotel features a tasteful and varied selection of *pupus* (appetizers) and an open bar. For those who really thrive on being out on the water, the sumptuous dinner sail and sunset cruise should not be missed.

Typical depth range	:	15–30 feet (5–10 meters)
Typical current conditions	:	Generally negligible much of the year
Expertise required	:	Novice
Access	:	Beach or boat

The Kona Surf Hotel is located just south of Keauhou Bay, opposite a most interesting diving area.

The Manta Ray Night Dive. Local dive shops and dive tour companies also offer boat dives to this site, and a very interesting night-dive package was started some years ago by Gold Coast Divers. It was so successful that other underwater tour companies joined in. It's called the manta ray night dive and, obviously, manta rays frequent this area. The Kona Surf is the largest hotel on the bay and shines powerful lights out onto the water that attract the great mantas if conditions, especially the weather, are right. The mantas follow their food source, microscopic plankton, which only come near the surface when there is little or no moon.

It is strongly recommended that you go with an organized dive tour to make the manta ray night dive. Not only will you be safer, but you will also have the best chance of seeing these graceful creatures on a guided tour. To jump into the dark night water and be surrounded by huge, gently finning manta rays is one of those experiences in life not likely to be repeated.

The masked butterfly fish is a quick-change artist. Here, it's seen in its daytime colors. As soon as the sun goes down, however, its color changes. The bright yellow on its body turns a dull grayish brown, giving it an uncanny resemblance to a racoon.

Kaiwi. There is, of course, no guarantee that manta rays will be seen on every dive. If they do not come around, this dive site is not particularly good as far as bottom terrain and marine life are concerned, and an alternate site will be chosen be the tour operators. Usually this alternate will be the south side of Kaiwi, a lovely spot for both day and night dives, though it can only be reached by boat. The area abounds in invertebrates, lobsters, and sleeping parrotfish, all set in a nice coral garden. In closer to shore the bottom is shallow, about 20 feet (6 meters) with interesting arches and caves and a shark cave that often contains reef and white-tip sharks. About 40 yards (37 meters) from shore the depth is 45 feet (12 meters), and then suddenly there is a dramatic drop-off which goes straight down into deep open ocean water. The area is full of fish life and is excellent for photography.

White tip sharks— also called white pointers—reside on a number of reefs around the islands. They're sometimes found on the sand bottom under a ledge.

Typical depth range	:	15–75 feet (5–23 meters)
Typical current conditions	:	Not a factor unless there is a south swell
Expertise required	:	Novice to advanced
Access	:	Beach

South of Kealakekua Bay is historic Honaunau, the City of Refuge park. It is so named because it served in ancient times as a sanctuary for criminals and warriors defeated in battle.

Honaunau Bay is a good spot for beach diving with good near-shore scenery. Drive past the restrooms and picnic area and park near the sandy beach, where you can cross a low lava-rock shelf for the best entry into the water. Two notes of caution here: Check local weather conditions to be certain the surf is down, and watch out for the sea urchins. Rubber booties or shoes are recommended for getting into and exiting the water.

The graceful lionfish, a member of the scorpion family, is beautiful but deadly. The feather-like spines on its back can be used to inject a powerful venom.

The jagged, horn-like beak of this parrotfish can be clearly seen. Parrotfish are essential to reef development. With their tough beaks, they scrape algae off of coral. Left alone, the algae would overgrow and kill the coral colonies.

In Hanaunau Bay itself, the bottom drops off fairly quickly. The shoreline is rugged, with arches and canyons that cut back into the shore and make for interesting exploration.

If you swim farther out into the bay, there is a steep ledge which drops off to about 150 feet (45 meters). The bay abounds with fish life.

Hanaunau Bay is a bit distant from Kona and thus not frequented by dive tours. Because it offers shore entry, it is recommended for those who wish to dive on their own rather than with an organized group. Before making the drive, check weather conditions with a local dive shop to be sure there is no south swell that could make diving dangerous. The skill level here ranges from novice to advanced, depending on whether you stay close to shore or venture further out into deeper water. Plan your dive according to your level of experience.

Typical depth range	:	15–75 feet (5–23 meters)
Typical current conditions	:	Not a factor unless there is a north swell
Expertise required	:	Novice to advanced
Access	:	Boat

Red Hill lies some 8 miles (13 kilometers) south of Kona, several hundred yards offshore. It is named after a distinctive, half-cinder cone which is now an extinct submerged crater. The dive area is actually a large bay approximately one half mile (1 kilometer) across.

Red Hill is one of the more popular dive sites in the Kona area. It is frequented daily by local divers and dive shop tours. Everybody has a favorite spot and almost anywhere is good. The cinder-cone crater is honeycombed with a series of remarkable shallow-water lava tubes. Some of these are as much as 10 feet (3 meters) in diameter, many illuminated along their entire length by shafts of sunlight shining through holes in the roof. The lava tubes average about 50 feet (15 meters) in depth; some are open at both ends while others are dead ends. Outside of the lava tubes are other lava rock formations offering varied scenery: canyonways, surge channels, pits, walls, ledges, drop-offs, and overhangs.

Fantasy Reef and Driftwood. Two areas within Red Hill are of particular note—Fantasy Reef and Driftwood, lying about 400 to 500 yards (370–462 meters) apart. Fantasy Reef has been linked to a fantasy land of undulating coral and lava rock hills with yellow and green plating corals, elkhorn and pink corals, and hovering schools of delicately painted butterflyfish, Morrish Idols, and curious blue-head wrasse. The main feature of Fantasy Reef is its labyrinthine network of canyons. The top of these canyons may be only 6 feet (2 meters) across on the top of the reef and descend 20 or 25 feet (6–18 meters) down into the rock. Like a maze, these canyons frequently branch off into other channels. It is really a remarkable place to explore.

Driftwood does not have the spectacular terrain that Fantasy Reef does, but the topography is quite interesting. It is actually an underwater peninsula that sticks out from shore and contains cave complexes. One of these is a shark cave where you have a 50/50 chance of coming across its small resident white-tip sharks.

Red Hill is best done as a two-tank dive; Fantasy Reef one dive, Driftwood the second.

Marine life of all types, such as this lemon butterfly fish, collects in the submerged crater of the extinct volcano at Red Hill. The area is honeycombed by lava tubes, canyons, pits and ledges. ▶

Typical depth range	:	20–90 feet (6–28 meters)
Typical current conditions	:	Generally non-existent most of the year
Expertise required	:	Novice
Access	:	Beach or boat

Kealakekua Bay is another spot of historic significance. Capt. James Cook, the discoverer of the Hawaiian Islands, was killed here in a battle with local islanders in 1779 hundreds of years ago.

Above water Kealakekua Bay offers a spectacular panorama of sheer, majestic volcanic cliffs honeycombed with ancient Hawaiian burial caves. On the other side of the bay is the quietly rural Hawaiian village of Napoopoo, where the islanders still fish just as their ancestors did.

A diver holds an inflated puffer fish in the marine park at Kealakekua Bay. Like the porcupine fish, the puffer swallows water when frightened, expanding itself like a balloon.

Unusual Marine Life. Kealakekua Bay is a protected underwater park, which means that nothing except pictures and memories can be taken out of the water. As a result, the 315 acre bay abounds with schools of tame tropical fish which are accustomed to being fed by visiting divers. Many other types of marine life prefer the sheltered waters of the bay, such as spotted eagle rays, gorgeously tinted nudibranchs, curious wrasse, butterflyfish, reclusive moral eels, and lots of coral. Kealakekua Bay is a popular place to bring visiting divers because of its sheltered waters, friendly fish, and beautiful underwater terrain.

If you are going to explore Kealakekua Bay on your own, the best water entry is on the Napoopoo side. There is a small beach park and shade trees where you can park. The clear water offers good skin and scuba diving quite close to shore for the novice. For the more hardy and experienced diver, a longer swim further out into the bay reveals rolling coral hills, clearer and deeper water, and even more fish life.

A number of dive tour boats bring visitors to Kealakekua Bay every day. Fish immediately flock to arriving boats and greet divers as they enter the water, hoping for a handout of bread. Kealakekua Bay is one of the nicest, easiest, and most conveniently dived spots on the Kona coast.

Convict tangs, named for their black-and-white striped coloration, are just one of the tame species to be found in the park at Kealakeua.

6

Diving in Kauai

Lying approximately 21 degrees north of the equator, the Hawaiian Islands are at the fringe of the warm water coral belt. Since Kauai is the northernmost island in the chain, corals flourish less in its waters than around the isles further south. Nonetheless, Kauai has an abundance of dive sites and some first-rate diving facilities. There are dive shops and dive tour companies in Kapaa, Hanalei, and Poipu.

The north shore, of course, catches more weather. It does have some excellent diving sites, but due to the sometimes quickly varying moods of wind and water, it is best to go with a dive tour to dive safely. The island's best, easiest, nearly year-round dive sites are found on the leeward southern shore. The beaches of Poipu are gorgeous and you will find the greatest variety of hotel and condo accommodations, as well as a plethora of dive shops, skin and scuba tour and equipment rental outfits.

Kauai is very lush, and noted for its tropical forests, and waterfalls. It is a popular pastime for visitors and natives alike.

DIVE SITE RATINGS

Kauai

	Novice Diver	Novice w/instructor or divemaster	Intermediate Diver	Intermediate w/instructor or divemaster	Advanced Diver	Advanced w/instructor or divemaster
1 Ke'e Lagoon*	×	×	×	×	×	×
2 Haena	×	×	×	×	×	×
3 Ahukini*			×	×	×	×
4 Koloa Landing	×	×	×	×	×	×
5 Poipu Beach	×	×	×	×	×	×

*Indicates good snorkeling spot.

When using the accompanying chart see the information on page 5 for an explanation of the diver rating system and site locations

Kauai is the place Hawaiians go to get away from it all. Although the northernmost island in the chain, and thus with less coral development, it offers some fine dive sites and relaxed, noncommercial atmosphere.

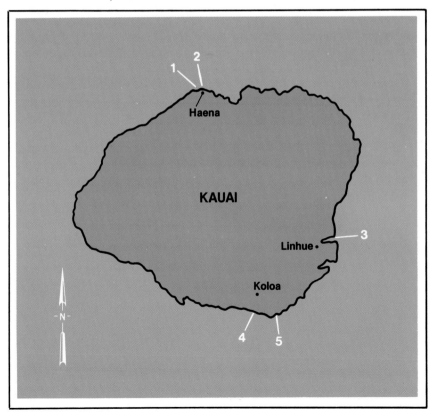

Typical depth range	:	10–20 feet (3–6 meters)
Typical current conditions	:	Steady current most of the year left along the beach; can be dangerous when strong. Much calmer to the right side of the lagoon
Expertise required	:	Novice to intermediate
Access	:	Beach

To begin with, remember that the north shore of Kauai, like the north shore of all islands, is calmest and safest during the summer months. Winter brings large surf and dangerous water conditions.

Scenic Ke'e Lagoon is found just to the west of Haena Beach Park. The lagoon itself is really too shallow for good scuba diving and is recommended for snorkelers or very novice scuba divers just getting used to the ocean. Depending on your level of experience, swim either to the left or the right; the right side is best for beginners, with a maximum depth of around 12 feet (4 meters). It is also calmer here. The terrain forms a channel as you swim to the right, running same distance along the shore. There are some interesting little ledges and fish life in this area.

To the left of the lagoon, within 50–70 yards (45–63 meters) of shore, the water gets down to 20 feet (6 meters) in depth. This area is recommended for the intermediate or advanced diver because of the presence of mild to strong currents. There are some nice ledges here and more abundant fish life than to the right side of the lagoon.

The visibility in the lagoon is generally good, about 40–60 feet (12–18 meters), weather dependent of course. The area is frequented by large schools of striped convict tangs known locally as *manini*. The bay is almost a fish nursery, and many juvenile species are seen here.

If the water is calm—and *only* if the water is calm—you can swim past the inner lagoon to the outer reef, where the diving is lovely. Depth averages 10–40 feet (3–12 meters); there is great visibility, caves, and a lot to see.

Inside the reef at Ke'e Lagoon, snorkelers find a varied seascape in water barely 20 feet (6 meters) deep. Outside the reef, the deeper water affords excellent visibility and caves and ledges to explore. ▶

Typical depth range	:	5–65 feet (2–20 meters)
Typical current conditions	:	Mild to strong at 20 feet (6 meters) or more
Expertise required	:	Novice to intermediate
Access	:	Beach

There are actually 2 dive sites at Haena, Cannon's reef and Tunnels reef as they are known locally.

Entry to Cannon's reef is best made through a V-shaped slit in the reef, which also makes a good exit point. It is 5–10 feet (2–3 meters) here. As you follow the ledge the water gets rapidly deeper, ultimately reaching 70 feet (21 meters) deep.

Bigeyes can be found hiding in the shelter of crevices and caves at Haena Beach.

The most extensive and most popular reef is Tunnels. The most convenient parking place is actually about a quarter mile (one half kilometer) to the right, or east, of Haena. Here you will find a dirt road running down to the water and a boat channel. Novice divers should swim to the right, where the channel fans out into a large sandy bottom pool surrounded by reef. The depth is about 7 feet (2 meters). From here you can swim further out as the sand bottom slopes gradually to a maximum depth of 25 feet (8 meters). There are some nice coral heads, caves, and fish life here.

The experienced diver should head out to the left of the channel. Here the sandy bottom slopes down to 65 feet (20 meters). Bear in mind that the deeper you go, the more pronounced the current becomes. There are some particularly nice ledges, caves, and overhangs in the 50-foot (15-meter) range. White-tip reef sharks are frequently sighted here.

A shallow bowl—a sandy bottom surrounded by reef—is one of the features of the Tunnels site in Haena Bay. Farther out, ledges, caves and overhands can be found in 50 feet (15 meters) of water. Lizardfish are often seen on the sand bottoms. Photo: B. Sastre.

Ahukini * 3

Typical depth range	:	15–45 feet (5–14 meters)
Typical current conditions	:	Very rough and dangerous most of year; but safe to dive during Kona weather
Expertise required	:	Intermediate
Access	:	Beach

One of the choicest of Kauai's dive sites is found on the windward side of the island, past the Lihue airport at the end of Ahukini Road (the road ends of Hanamaula Bay).

Unfortunately, most of the year this area is undiveable due to northwest tradewinds that hit the coastline with pounding surf. On those few days out of the year when the southerly Kona winds are blowing, this area becomes calm and the diving is excellent.

The disc butterfly fish is just one of the gracefully-colored tropical species that draws divers to Hawaii.

Nudibrances similar to this one perched on the diver's finger are often seen at Ahukini. Note the "gills" of the creature extended from its back. Photo: B. Sastre.

The dive site is past a large rock jetty on the far right side of the bay. This jetty served as the pier for the old harbor before the new one was built at Nawiliwili. Entry can be made, if the water is really calm, directly over the rocks in front of the pier.

Once out to the dive site, the visibility is almost always good, 60–80 feet (18–25 meters) and more. There is a wide variety of reef shapes for interesting topography and exploration. The marine life is equally varied— lobster and crabs, fish, nudibranchs, and lots more. This is also a fairly regular stopping-off place for the humpback whale during the winter migrations, and divers have actually been able to touch these gentle giants during dives. When the weather is right, it's a great spot.

Koloa Landing 4

Typical depth range	:	10–40 feet (3–12 meters)
Typical current conditions	:	None
Expertise required	:	Novice to intermediate
Access	:	Beach

Halfway between Koloa and Poipu beach is a sheltered cove that is excellent for diving. This is Koloa Landing. A popular boat landing, Koloa is perhaps the favorite dive site on Kauai's south shore. It is a well-protected cove, and even when all other parts of the island are undiveable due to poor weather, this site is almost always calm. The cove features a large variety of corals, and the fish here are quite used to divers dropping in on them and are thus very tame, easily hand fed, and very photogenic. The most common of these friendly finned creatures is the attractive blue-stope snapper, which has an affinity for being hand fed. Curious saddle-back wrasse are also abundant.

There are two dive spots within the cove, to the right and to the left. The left side is a bit more barren, but it does have some nice corals and fish, although it is not nearly as attractive as the right side. The right side is the most popular among local divers and dive tours. In addition to fish and coral formations, it features some very tame moray eels. George and Hermi, for instance, are always about to greet divers, and are so accustomed to humans that they can be hand fed.

Photogenic fish, such as this parrot fish, are used to being fed and photographed at Koloa Landing. Both divers and snorkelers are able to explore the shallow coral formations.

Typical depth range	:	5–40 feet (2–12 meters)
Typical current conditions	:	Not a factor in the cove; mild currents may exist outside the cove
Expertise required	:	Novice to intermediate
Access	:	Beach

Poipu Beach Park is east of Koloa Landing, adjacent to the Waiohai Hotel. Poipu Beach is probably the best spot on the island of Kauai for the beginning snorkeler and scuba diver; novices can enjoy the underwater world in complete safety and comfort here. There is rarely any kind of current, even a mild one, in the cove itself. Even on the outside only mild currents have been reported.

There are a number of tide pools on one side of the cove. To the left of these pools the water is only 3–5 feet (1–2 meters) deep, and this is a good place for beginners to get their feet wet. From here you can swim out until the water becomes 10–20 feet (3–6 meters) deep; outside the cove depths average 30–40 feet (10–12 meters). The cove is frequented daily by dive shops and skin diving tour companies. The fish are thus very accustomed to visitors and have become extremely tame and they are easily hand fed.

The fish at Poipu Beach are also well-accustomed to humans and very tame. Poipu has almost no current, and with its shallow tide pools, makes an excellent spot for beginning snorkelers to try out their fins and snorkels.

7

Safety

This section discusses common hazards, including dangerous marine animals, and emergency procedures in case of a diving accident. We do not discuss the diagnosis or treatment of serious medical problems; refer to your first aid manual or emergency diving accident manual for that information.

Diving Accidents

The Divers Alert Network (DAN), a membership association of individuals and organizations sharing a common interest in diving safety operates a **24 hour national hotline (919) 684-8111** (collect calls are accepted in an emergency). DAN does not directly provide medical care, however they do provide advice on early treatment, evacuation and hyperbaric treatment of diving related injuries. Additionally, DAN provides diving safety information to members to help prevent accidents. Membership is $10 a year, offering: the DAN *Underwater Diving Accident Manual*, describing symptoms and first aid for the major diving related injuries, emergency room physician guidelines for drugs and i.v. fluids; a membership card listing diving related symptoms on one side and DAN's emergency and non emergency phone numbers on the other; 1 tank decal and 3 small equipment decals with DAN's logo and emergency number; and a newsletter, "Alert Diver" describes diving medicine and safety information in layman's language with articles for professionals, case histories, and medical questions related to diving. Special memberships for dive stores, dive clubs, and corporations are also available. The DAN Manual can be purchased for $4 from the Administrative Coordinator, National Diving Alert Network, Duke University Medical Center, Box 3823, Durham, NC 27710.

DAN divides the U.S. into 7 regions, each coordinated by a specialist in diving medicine who has access to the skilled hyperbaric chambers in his region. Non emergency or information calls are connected to the DAN office and information number, (919) 684-2948. This number can be dialed direct, between 9 A.M. and 5 P.M. Monday-Friday Eastern Standard time. Divers should *not* call DAN for chamber locations. Chamber status changes frequently making this kind of information dangerous if obsolete at the time of an emergency. Instead, divers should contact DAN as soon

Emergency Services

Oahu
Hospitals:
Queen's Medical Center
1301 Punchbowl,
538-9011.
Diving Doctors:
call U.S. Navy Hyperbaric facility at
Submarine Base,
Pearl Harbor,
422-5955.
Recompression Facilities:
Submarine Base, Pearl Harbor,
422-5955.
Police: 911.

Big Island
Hospitals:
Hilo Hospital
1190 Waianuenue Ave.,
961-4211.
Diving Doctors:
contact Coast Guard,
536-4336.
Recompression Facilities:
call Coast Guard for evacuation to Honolulu,
Pearl Harbor, 536-4336.
Police:
935-3311, Hilo;
323-2645, Kona.

Maui
Hospitals:
Maui Memorial
221 Mahalani St.,
Wailuku, Maui, 244-9056.
Diving Doctors:
Steven Strong
Kaiser Medical Clinic
502 Pavoa Rd.,
Lahaina, 661-0081.
Recompression Facilities:
Maui Memorial
244-9056.
Police: 911.

Kauai
Hospitals:
G.N. Wilcox Memorial Hospital
3420 Kuhio Hwy.,
245-4811.
Diving Doctors:
U.S. Navy Hyperbaric Facility
Pearl Harbor, Honolulu,
422-5955.
Recompression Facilities:
call Coast Guard for Evacuation to Honolulu,
Pearl Harbor, 536-4336.
Police: 911.

as a diving emergency is suspected. All divers should have comprehensive medical insurance and check to make sure that hyperbaric treatment and air ambulance services are covered internationally.

Diving is a safe sport and there are very few accidents compared to the number of divers and number of dives made each year. But when the infrequent injury does occur, DAN is ready to help. DAN, originally 100% federally funded, is now largely supported by the diving public. Membership in DAN or purchase of DAN manuals or decals provides divers with useful safety information and provides DAN with necessary operating funds. Donations to DAN are a deductible as DAN is a legal non-profit public service organization.

Dangerous Marine Animals

Sea Urchins. As in the rest of the world, the most common hazardous animal that divers will encounter in the Hawaiian Islands is the long-spined sea urchin. This urchin has spines that can penetrate wetsuits, booties, and gloves. Injuries are nearly always immediately painful, and sometimes infect. Urchins are found at every diving depth, although they are more common in shallow water near shore, especially under coral heads. At night the urchins come out of their hiding places and are even easier to bump into. Minor injuries can be treated by extracting the spines (it's worth a try, though they're hard to get out) and treating the wound with antibiotic cream; make sure your tetanus immunization is current. Usually, spine bits fester and pop out several weeks later. Some people feel that crushing an embedded spine will make it dissolve faster in the tissues. Serious punctures will require a doctor's attention.

Barracudas. Barracudas are not commonly seen in Hawaiian waters, and are included in this section only because of their undeserved reputation for ferocity. If you do see barracudas, they will often get close enough to be at the edge of visibility.

Sting Rays. Sting rays can be seen in sand flats. They do not attack, but they don't like being sat on, stepped on, or prodded. They often are partially covered with sand, so look before you settle down on sandy bottoms. The long barbed stinger at the base of the tail can inflict a serious wound. Wounds are always extremely painful, often deep and infective, and can cause serious symptoms including anaphylactic shock. If you get stung, head for the hospital and let a doctor take care of the wound.

Scorpionfishes. Scorpionfish are well camouflaged, usually less than a foot (30 centimeters) long, and have poisonous spines hidden among their fins. They are often difficult to spot because they typically sit quietly on the bottom, looking more like plant-covered rocks than live fish. As with sting rays, watch where you put your hands and knees and you're not likely to meet one the hard way. If you get stung, severe allergic reactions are quite possible and great pain and infection are possible depending on the species. Head for the hospital and see a doctor.

Lionfish. Lionfish are in the same family as scorpionfish, but instead of lying camouflaged on the bottom, these fish can be seen quietly drifting along the reef, usually, at night. They should not be touched as their sting can be quite serious.

Sharks. The most common sharks seen on the Hawaiian reefs are the sandbar shark, the black tip, and the Galapagos shark. The sandbar shark usually flees when it sees a diver, the other two are more curious. Often they swim close to investigate divers and then swim away. When any shark begins to hang around it is best to leave the water.

Eels. Moray eels are dangerous only if harassed. There are lots of morays under coral heads and in crevices, and cornered eels will bite. Feeding and fondling morays is not recommended. If you get nipped, bites are sometimes infective and very painful and call for a doctor's attention.

The beautiful lionfish is graceful but deadly. The feather like spines on its back can be used to inject a powerful venom.

Appendix I

Dive Shops

Oahu

Aaron's Dive Shop,
39 Malunui Ave.,
Kailua, 261-1211.

Aloha Dive Shop,
Koko Marina Center,
395-8882.

American Dive Hawaii,
3684 Waialae Ave.,
Honolulu, 732-2877.

Bojac's,
Westgate Center,
Waipahu, 671-0311.

Hawaiian Divers,
2344 Kam Hwy.,
Honolulu, 845-6644.

Hawaii Sea Adventures,
98-316 Kam Hwy.,
Pearl City, 487-7515.

Sea Urchins Scuba Shop
98-025 Hekaha St.,
Aiea, 487-9060.

Rainbow Divers
1652 Wilikina Dr.
Wahiawa, 622-4532

Dan's Dive Shop,
660 Ala Moana Ave.,
Honolulu, 536-6181.
South Seas Aquatics,
Ward Warehouse,
Honolulu, 538-3854.
Scuba Shop,
Sand Island Access Rd.,
Honolulu, 845-4561.
Pacific Quest
46-216 Kahuhipa St.
Kaneohe, 235-3877
Waikiki Diving,
420 Nahua St.,
Honolulu, 922-7188.
Steve's Diving Adventures,
1700 Ala Moana Blvd.,
Honolulu, 947-8900.
Leeward Dive Center,
85-979 Farrington Hwy.,
Waianae, 696-3414.

Maui

Central Pacific Divers,
780 Front St.,
661-8718, Lahaina.
Kihei Sea Sports,
Kihei Town Center,
Kihei, 879-1919.
Scuba Schools of Maui,
1000 Limahana,
Lahaina, 661-8036.
Skin Diving Maui,
2411 S. Kihei Rd.,
Kihei, 879-1502.
American Dive,
628 Front St.,
Lahaina, 661-4885.
Hawaiian Reef Divers,
129 Lahainaluna Rd.,
Lahaina, 667-7647.
Maui Dive Shop,
Azeka Place,
Kihei, 879-3388.
Lahaina Divers,
710 Front St.,
Lahaina, 661-8610.
Dive Maui,
Lahaina Marketplace,
Lahailuna Rd.,
Lahaina, 667-2080.

Ocean Activities Center,
Wailea Town Center,
Kihei, 879-4487.
Kaanapali Divers,
Lahaina, 661-4411.
The Dive Shop,
Kihei Rd.,
Kihei, 879-5172.

Hawaii

Gold Coast Divers,
King Kam Hotel,
Kona, 329-1328.
Jack's Diving Locker,
Kona, 329-7585.
Nautilus Dive Center,
382 Kam Ave.,
Hilo, 935-6939.
Ocean Sports Hawaii,
885-6064.
Kona Reef Divers,
325-5555.
Kona Coast Skin Divers,
Kona, 329-8802.
Dive Makai,
Kona, 329-2025.

Kauai

Fathom Five Divers,
Koloa, 742-6991.
Ocean Odyssey,
4-363 Kuhio Hwy.,
Kapaa, 822-9680.
Aquatics Kauai,
733 Kuhio Hwy.,
Kapaa, 822-9213.
Napali Zodiac,
Hanalei, 826-9371.
Sea Sage Diving Center,
4-1378 Kuhio Hwy.,
Kapaa, 822-3841.

Index

YOU NEED DAN
DAN NEEDS YOU!

Join the
DIVERS ALERT
NETWORK

DAN FILLS A NEED

DAN unites hyperbaric chamber facilities into a nationwide communications network to help divers and their physicians arrange consultation, transportation, and treatment by using a single central emergency telephone number.

FOR DIVING EMERGENCIES CALL (919) 684-8111
24 HOURS   7 DAYS A WEEK
FOR INFORMATION CALL **(919) 684-2948** MONDAY-FRIDAY 9-5 E.S.T.

DAN NEEDS YOU

The cost of providing this invaluable national service is high. Startup funding was provided by the federal government but not continued. Do your part by becoming a member of DAN which will help insure the continuing existence of DAN as well as provide you with **diving safety information.**

JOINING DAN — $10

Individual membership in Dan is $10 per year — a small sum to insure there will be somebody able to help you immediately in the event of an accident.
On joining you will receive:
- **MEMBERSHIP CARD** with the DAN phone number and a list of diving injury symptoms.
- **TANK DECALS** with the DAN emergency phone number.
- The DAN **UNDERWATER DIVING ACCIDENT MANUAL** which describes symptoms and first aid for the major diving related injuries plus guidelines a physician can follow for drugs and i.v. fluid administration.
- A NEWSLETTER, "ALERT DIVER", presents information on diving medicine and diving safety. Actual DAN case histories and questions are presented in each issue.

☐ Yes. I wish to join the National Divers Alert Network (DAN), and enclose my membership fee of $10. Please send my new member's package as soon as is possible. (Please allow 3-6 weeks for delivery.)

☐ I am enclosing an extra tax deductible donation of $ _____

CORPORATE MEMBERS
Tax deductible corporate membership is encouraged. Please write for more information.

——— Supporting Organizations ———
NASDS • NAUI • PADI • SSI • USA • YMCA

NAME _____

ADDRESS _____

_____

AGENCY _____
Check if you are a:
☐ instructor   ☐ dive shop operator   ☐ physician

Mail to: **DIVERS ALERT NETWORK**
BOX 3823 • DUKE UNIVERSITY MEDICAL CENTER
DURHAM, NORTH CAROLINA 27710

Collect all 12 Pisces Diving and Snorkeling Guides:

The Virgin Islands
The Bahamas
Bonaire
The Cayman Islands
The Channel Islands
Cozumel

The Family Islands and Grand Bahama
Northern California
Southern California
The Hawaiian Islands
The Florida Keys
Florida's East Coast

DIVING AND SNORKELING GUIDE TO **The Hawaiian Islands**

The **DIVING AND SNORKELING GUIDE TO THE HAWAIIAN ISLANDS** contains detailed descriptions of some of the best dive sites on the breathtakingly beautiful islands of Hawaii, Kauai, Oahu, and Maui, including Honaunau Bay, Kealakekua Bay, Ahukini, Poipu Beach, Magic Island, the Blowhole, Rainbow Reef, Molokini Crater, and Lanai Island. You'll also find useful information on the many topside attractions of these fabulous islands.

All the Pisces **DIVING AND SNORKELING GUIDES** have been compiled and edited by a group of experts who know exactly the kind of information you need to make your diving or snorkeling vacation a safe and totally enjoyable experience.

Every guide is written by an authority on the region and illustrated with maps and beautiful underwater and topside photographs. Each dive site listed in the book is described in detail, with specific information on:

- **Type of dive**
- **Approximate depth**
- **Presence and strength of currents**
- **Accessibility**
- **Required diving expertise**

- **Type of bottom terrain**
- **Typical marine life you can expect to encounter**
- **Special points of interest**

In addition to the individual site descriptions, tables in each book rate all the sites in terms of diver experience, so you can tell at a glance whether or not a particular dive site is appropriate for you. The tables also point out especially good sites for snorkeling or night diving.

Other features of these informative guides include:

- **Maps showing local dive site locations**
- **Information on hotels and dive operations**
- **Local geography and natural history**
- **Emergency contacts, both local and U.S. mainland**

Whether you're in the planning stages of a vacation or in the middle of it, you will find these beautifully illustrated and highly informative guides of invaluable assistance.

About the Author

DOUG WALLIN, a writer and photographer, is a resident of Hawaii, and an authority on diving in the islands. His work as a photographer-writer has been widely published.

See last page for other Pisces Diving and Snorkeling Guides.

ISBN 1-55992-003-3

PISCES BOOKS
A Division of Gulf Publishing Company
P.O. Box 2608 • Houston, Texas 77252-2608

0 49764 92003 2